NEW DOMAINS
of EDUCATIONAL
LEADERSHIP

Leora Cruddas

With chapters by
Steve Rollett, Ben Newmark and Tom Rees,
and James Townsend and Ed Vainker

hachette
LEARNING

To order, please visit www.HachetteLearning.com or contact Customer Service at education@hachette.co.uk / +44 (0)1235 827827.

ISBN: 978 1 0360 1047 8

© Leora Cruddas 2025

First published in 2025 by
Hachette Learning,
An Hachette UK Company
Carmelite House
50 Victoria Embankment
London EC4Y 0DZ
www.HachetteLearning.com

The authorised representative in the EEA is Hachette Ireland, 8 Castlecourt Centre, Dublin, D15 XTP3, Ireland (email: info@hbgi.ie)

Impression number   10 9 8 7 6 5 4 3 2 1

Year   2029 2028 2027 2026 2025

Illustrations by DC Graphic Design Limited
Typeset in the UK.
Printed in the UK.

A catalogue record for this title is available from the British Library.

MIX
Paper | Supporting
responsible forestry
FSC
www.fsc.org   FSC™ C104740

Leora Cruddas is the founding Chief Executive of the Confederation of School Trusts (CST) – the national organisation and sector body for school trusts in England. She has advised successive governments and sits on several Department for Education advisory bodies. She also sits on the advisory body for Evidence Based Education, is a fellow of the RSA and a member of the Institute of Directors.

Prior to founding CST, she was Director of Policy and Public Relations for the Association of School and College Leaders (ASCL). Leora has six years' of experience as a director of education in two London local authorities.

She is a visiting professor at UCL Institute of Education.

Leora was made a CBE in the New Year's Honours in 2022.

LEARNING

Together we unlock every learner's unique potential

At Hachette Learning (formerly Hodder Education), there's one thing we're certain about. No two students learn the same way. That's why our approach to teaching begins by recognising the needs of individuals first.

Our mission is to allow every learner to fulfil their unique potential by empowering those who teach them. From our expert teaching and learning resources to our digital educational tools that make learning easier and more accessible for all, we provide solutions designed to maximise the impact of learning for every teacher, parent and student.

Aligned to our parent company, Hachette Livre, founded in 1826, we pride ourselves on being a learning solutions provider with a global footprint.

www.hachettelearning.com

ACKNOWLEDGEMENTS

There are so many people to thank. I'd like to start with Steve Munby CBE, whose wise counsel in the early days helped me navigate through a difficult time. Colleagues who have pushed the boundaries of my thinking: Lucy Heller, who gave me the courage to know that I could create Confederation of School Trusts; Sir Jon Coles, who makes me think hard about institutional architecture; Sir Nick Weller, who reminds me of the power of the trust sector as a disruptive force, with its focus on doing things differently and better for schools and pupils from economically disadvantaged communities; Susan Douglas CBE, for her inspirational leadership of special schools; Tom Rees, who has helped me to think so deeply about the SEND system; Luke Sparkes, for helping me think about strategy and culture; Jenny Thompson and Funmilola Stewart, whose thinking about social justice is always inspirational and educative; Ed Vainker OBE, who has taught me so much about the importance of community; Dawn Haywood, who embodies civic partnership; Sir Hamid Patel, for his enduring wisdom; Clare Robson-Farrelly, who has been there since the beginning and helped me to build CST; Sir David Carter, for his early leadership of the trust movement, and his support and friendship. The people who helped me shape this book and gave me feedback: Steve Rollett (whose leadership of CST with me is so important), Tom Rees and Charis Evans. Every single one of the case study contributors and the colleagues who authored and co-authored chapters, who have all challenged the horizons of my thinking. Professor Becky Francis CBE, Hilary Spencer and Dr Kate Chhatwal OBE, for their enduring colleagueship and friendship. My wonderful leadership group and board of trustees, who challenge me to be the best that I can be, and whose protective wisdom and leadership has ensured the success of CST. Finally, CST members whose courage and fortitude impress me every single day. Thank you for everything you do. It is a privilege to represent you.

CONTENTS

Foreword: Sir Hamid Patel CBE..9

Introduction 11

PART 1: TRUST LEADERSHIP

Chapter 1:   Leading the organisation..31

Chapter 2:   Advancing education: the DNA of trust-led school
improvement (by Steve Rollett) 44

Chapter 3:   Advancing education: five principles for inclusion
(by Ben Newmark and Tom Rees) 67

Chapter 4:   Strategic governance..84

Chapter 5:   Operations and workforce...101

PART 2: CIVIC LEADERSHIP

Chapter 6:   The trust as a civic institution 123

Chapter 7:   Building a connected system...136

Chapter 8:   Catalysing collective leadership through a theory of action..144

Chapter 9:   The protection and promotion of public values 154

Chapter 10:   Community anchoring (by James Townsend, Ed Vainker
and Leora Cruddas) 169

PART 3: SYSTEM LEADERSHIP

Chapter 11:   Building the narrative: why a trust-led system? 185

Chapter 12:   System building: acting *on*, rather than just acting *in*
the system 195

Chapter 13:   Curating the pipeline of the next generation of leaders..208

Chapter 14:   Creating the conditions for the system to keep getting better..217

Chapter 15:   Building public institutions..230

Afterword: An open letter to school and trust leaders 237

FOREWORD

Power is the ability to achieve purpose.

Martin Luther King Jnr

Over the last two decades, trusts have assumed an increasingly significant role as education providers. In January 2024, 44.2% of primary school pupils, 81.7% of secondary school pupils and 43.6% of special school pupils attended academies or free schools, figures that will continue to increase.

It is the responsibility of trust leaders to show that the faith and investment placed in us yields positive outcomes.

The skills required of trust leadership are complex and multifaceted. In this comprehensive study, three domains are given close consideration: organisational leadership, civic leadership and system leadership. If we are to maximise our opportunities and powers as trust leaders, we must attend closely to all three elements, securing our foundations and extending our influence.

Our trusts communicate strong moral integrity, focused on driving up standards and ensuring better life chances for every child and young person in our care. This is our fundamental, essential mission.

We cannot achieve this alone.

We know that the factors impinging on the lives of our pupils and their families require radical multi-agency solutions. The time has come for us to be the architects and drivers of change, using the powers invested in us to do things differently.

This book offers insights into how trusts can operate *on* rather than *in* the system, to shape the future. It combines theoretical discourse on the new domains of educational leadership with practical case studies illustrating how civic responsibility can be realised and how the education sector as a whole can be strengthened by agile, innovative and principled trusts.

I hope that you find affirmation and inspiration in the chapters that follow.

Our time is now.

Sir Hamid Patel CBE
Chair of the Confederation of School Trusts

INTRODUCTION

Let me start by telling you a little bit about myself. A big part of my professional identity is as an English teacher. I was born and educated in Apartheid South Africa. There is a whole story there, but it is not the story of this book. I started my teaching career in the 'township' of Alexandra, in a school that ran from a community hall, funded by non-governmental organisations. I learned so much from working in this community: I learned of people's anger and their struggle, the grinding poverty of daily life and their belief in education, their huge cultural wealth. This was the place where the poet Mongane Wally Serote and the writer Mark Mathabane grew up. It was also the place where a young Nelson Mandela rented a room when he first came to Johannesburg in 1941. My professional self, and much of what I believe about education, leadership and social justice, was forged in these years.

When I finished my master's degree at the University of the Witwatersrand, I had the privilege of coming to teach in England. I arrived in the year that Tony Blair's Labour government was formed. I came to teach in the London Borough of Newham because, at that time, it had a reputation for leading the thinking on inclusive education. I was seconded to the local authority as a special educational needs advisor and then continued to work for local government for a long time, ending up as director of education in Waltham Forest and then in Harrow.

I left local government to work at the Association of School and College Leaders (ASCL), the trade union and professional association for school and college leaders. It was there that I first saw the need for an organisation to represent the emerging sector of academy trusts. An academy trust in England is an organisation that is set up purely for the purposes of running schools. It is a charity, usually with a single charitable 'object' or purpose:

to advance education for public benefit.[1] The majority of academy trusts in England are multi-school organisations. In this aspect, the trust structure is somewhat comparable to 'stichtingen' in the Netherlands or charter school organisations in the United States.

I was aware that other 'sector bodies' representing public organisations existed – for example, the Association of Colleges, which was established in the mid-1990s when further education colleges in England were 'incorporated' and left local authority control. I also knew about the NHS Confederation, the sector body and membership organisation that brings together, supports and speaks for the healthcare system.

So, working with a board of trustees, I created the blueprint for the Confederation of School Trusts (CST) – the sector body and membership organisation for school trusts in England. At the time of writing (August 2024), CST is six years old and represents around three-quarters of all academy schools in England.

The genesis of this book

I first thought about the subject of the domains of leadership over the Christmas holidays in December 2019, a little over a year after CST was formed. It seemed to me then that the pressures on the school system were so profound that it was beyond the reach of individual institutions to respond, if our children are to flourish. Back then, I thought we needed to think about a new mental model of leadership to respond to these challenges, so I spent the Christmas holidays writing about three nested narratives of education leadership:

---

1   The exception is Catholic trusts, where the charitable object is as follows: '4(a) The Company's objects are specifically restricted to the advancement of the Catholic religion in the Diocese by such means as the Diocesan Bishop may think fit and proper by, but without prejudice to the generality of the foregoing, the establishing, maintaining, carrying on, managing and developing of Catholic schools in the United Kingdom conducted in accordance with the principles, and subject to the regulations and discipline of the Catholic Church. 4(b) Subject to the approval of the Diocesan Bishop [and Religious Superior], during the period that the objects in 4(a) are being fulfilled and form the majority of the activities of the Company, the advancement of education by the establishing, maintaining, carrying on, managing and developing of schools which are not Catholic in the United Kingdom.'

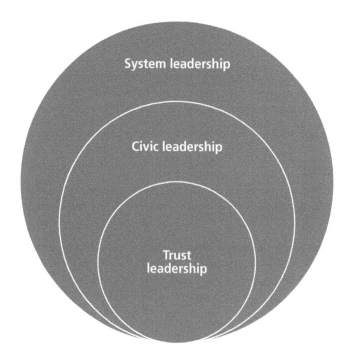

Trust leadership

The first narrative is about leadership of the organisation: the school trust. I do not use the word MAT (which is the acronym for multi-academy trust) because I think it is ugly, and parents do not understand what it means. It cannot therefore be the basis for building the future of our education system. Parents send their children to a school, so I use the term 'school trust'. The majority of school trusts are groups of schools working in deep and purposeful collaboration in a single legal entity, under strong, strategic governance.

Trust leaders must have a deep knowledge and understanding of the substance of education, including:

- schools and how to improve them
- organisations and how to build them
- people and how to develop them
- finances and how to manage them.

The primary leadership task is about creating high-quality education through developing expertise in curriculum and teaching across the group of schools in a financially sustainable way.

But there is a wider consideration beyond the knowledge and competence of trust leaders to lead their organisation. We must put at the heart of our reform journey this simple and powerful purpose – that education is a public good.

Leadership of our organisation is therefore necessary, but not sufficient.

Civic leadership

I thought back in 2019 that if our children are to flourish, we need to work with other civic leaders for a wider common good. I started to use the language of civic leadership.

Earlier that year, I felt really honoured to be invited to give evidence to the UPP Foundation Civic University Commission. It was a privilege to have the opportunity to think hard about the civic role of universities and the role they play in their localities by making a strategic contribution to the greater social good.

This experience led me to think that civic leadership is not the sole purview of locally elected politicians. It is enacted by many different civic structures, including, but not limited to, local government.

Civic leadership is different from community leadership. Community leader is a designation for a person widely perceived to represent a community. Civic leadership is about the protection and promotion of public values and addressing issues of place or public concern.

In talking to the Civic University Commission, I realised that school trusts are civic organisations too – just like universities and indeed NHS trusts – so I started to talk about 'civic trusts' and about trust leaders as civic leaders who create the conditions for collective impact by addressing complex issues affecting children and young people that require different actors to work together.

As well as leading a group of schools, trust leaders also look out beyond their organisation, and work with other civic leaders. But even this, although entirely necessary, I thought was still not sufficient.

System leadership

This brought me to the third of the nested narratives: system leadership. I defined system leadership back then as acting *on*, not just *in* the school system. I still think this is the right definition of system leadership.

I worried back then (and I still worry) that sometimes we are beset by a compliance mindset – we wait for governments to determine the policy context, then usually we rail against it, and mostly we then comply with it. This is acting *in* the system.

I believe acting *on* the system gives us an opportunity to think differently. We should think of leadership as the ability to shape the system.

Another way of thinking about this is to use Michael Fullan and Joanne Quinn's definition of 'systemness' (Fullan and Quinn, 2015). What they mean by this is the importance of focusing direction, and the need to integrate what the system is doing. Right now, in England, the system is building groups of schools.

The concept of the independent organisation set up purely for the purpose of running and improving schools has been part of the policy of all three main political parties – the Labour administration pre-2010, the coalition government (Conservatives and Liberal Democrats) between 2010 and 2015, and successive Conservative administrations since 2015.

The academies 'model' introduced by the Labour Government in 2002 was focused on poorly performing secondary schools in more deprived urban areas. The coalition government's 2010 Academies Act made it possible for 'good' and 'outstanding' state schools to convert to become academies and form groups of schools. Both types of academies are state-funded schools which are independent of local authorities. As noted above, I refer to academy trusts as school trusts, to reflect their core education purpose.

At the time of writing, more than half of children and young people are now educated in school trusts, and more than half of state schools in England are in trusts.

We should work together now to build the resilience of our school system to invite all schools to join a group of schools working together in a trust. To return to Fullan and Quinn, we should build system coherence. We should not wait for governments to do this. We can do this by the power of our argument, which I explore in chapter eleven. We can be the system architects.

The advent of the global pandemic

In January 2020, I published a paper that was the first articulation of the domains, called back then 'Systems of meaning: three nested leadership narratives' (Cruddas, 2020). At the time, I had no idea that, in less than eight weeks, we would face one of the greatest challenges in living history: the Covid-19 global pandemic.

On the evening of 18 March 2020, after speaking personally to the then Secretary of State for Education, I wrote the following message to CST members:

> Good evening Colleagues,
>
> I am writing following the Secretary of State's statement in the House.
>
> As you know I have been working closely with him, senior civil servants and regulators.
>
> I will start by saying there is no precedent, within our lifetimes, for the decisions that the Government is having to make. Mass school closures could have the effect of collapsing the NHS, leading to a substantial civic crisis on top of a public health emergency. The mass closure of schools would have a huge impact on the economy and would mean that many parents – front-line workers and those in the so-called gig economy – could not work. The impact of this on children and young people – on food poverty, safeguarding and welfare – is huge.
>
> In this time of national emergency, I hope you will feel able to support the decisions that the Government is taking in relation to schools. Of course, not all CST members will agree personally with the decisions that have been made. Many of you have said to me that the Government should set out its expectations of schools and leaders very clearly – and then you will step up to those expectations. Now is the hour to do this.
>
> Schools are education institutions. But in this hour of need, we will need schools to limit provision from Monday to a basic level of care for the most vulnerable and the children of front-line workers. Front-line workers means health workers, the police service and the fire service, but it also means those who are involved in food supply and other basic services.
>
> As we face the coming weeks and months, it is likely that the supply of staff will wax and wane. Trusts are perhaps the most resilient of school structures and we will be relying on you to use your organisational resilience to support other local schools. This is the time for civic

leadership – for trusts to work with other civic actors to ensure that provision is in place.

There will be a coordinated approach to providing free school meals. As a minimum the DfE will contract to do this. And we will work with them to manage this.

Perhaps the most controversial of decisions announced today relates to public tests and exams. There will be no primary assessment. GCSEs and A-levels will be awarded on the basis of moderated assessment with the exam boards and Ofqual. Of course this is not ideal. But I am persuaded there is no better option. For those young people who feel that they could have done better than their predicted grade, I believe there will be mini-sessions in the autumn.

The messages to young people will need to be done with thought and care. Many young people and their parents will be upset and disappointed. Some will be angry. This is hard to understand. I know you will manage this with your usual aplomb, giving assurances in these extraordinary circumstances.

I will continue to work with the Secretary of State and his senior advisors over the coming days and weeks to map and coordinate the many details that flow from decisions made today. Please continue to let me know the issues you are – and will be – facing in your trusts.

The next meeting with the Secretary of State is likely to be Friday. Please do continue to send me your thoughts directly.

In this hour of need, I know I can rely on you to be the best that we can be.

The English teacher in me finds solace in poetry.

To everything there is a season, and a time to every purpose under the heaven:

A time to be born, and a time to die; a time to plant, and a time to pluck up that which is planted;

A time to kill, and a time to heal; a time to break down, and a time to build up;

A time to weep, and a time to laugh; a time to mourn, and a time to dance;

A time to cast away stones, and a time to gather stones together; a time to embrace, and a time to refrain from embracing;

A time to seek, and a time to lose; a time to keep, and a time to cast away;

A time to rend, and a time to sew; a time to keep silence, and a time to speak;

A time to love, and a time to hate; a time for war, and a time for peace.

King James Bible (Ecclesiastes 3:1)

In this time – in this season – we will step up.

Warmest wishes,

Leora

Like everyone else, I had no idea then of the longevity of this global crisis or the multiple negative impacts it would have – legacies we are still living with. I knew only this: that trusts were perhaps the most resilient of school structures and that we would be relying on trust leaders, working with local authorities, to use their organisational resilience to support other local schools. I said then, this is the time for civic leadership – for trusts to work with other civic actors to ensure that provision is in place.

In the months and years that followed, the three nested leadership narratives stood the test of time. Trust leaders began to use the language of civic leadership, and it is a more prominent part of the educational conversation about England's schools today.

Global shifts and challenges following the pandemic

The pandemic left us with multiple challenges, but we could not have anticipated those that followed: a global economic crisis, climate disasters, social unrest, global political instability, and conflicts and wars. These challenges are likely to determine our future.

The leadership challenge has become even more acute. My instinct in that Christmas period of 2019, that we needed a different mental model for leadership of our public institutions, became heightened. It is now clearer than ever it was that leadership of public institutions requires a different mental model.

So, I returned to my January 2020 paper (Cruddas, 2020) and rewrote it for a post-pandemic context. I called it 'The new domains of educational leadership' (Cruddas, 2023c). And that thinking is the basis for this book.

A duty of care

Following the pandemic, in 2022, Professor Peter Hennessy published an important book, *A Duty of Care: Britain Before and After Covid* (Hennessy, 2022). In it, he argues that what defined us in the post-Second World War period was our sense of a duty of care. This was the basis of the great reforms outlined in the Beveridge Report of 1942, which in turn resulted in the great pillars of the welfare state.

We rediscovered an intense duty of care throughout the pandemic. Hennessy refers to the Covid Inquiry and suggests that its report should be called '"It took a Virus ..." for this is what stimulated us collectively to sharpen and extend our sense of a duty of care for the vulnerable and those who are on the margins of society'.

I read this deeply important book before the CST annual conference in June 2022. I said in my conference speech, 'It may not be possible to enshrine into law the kindness we encountered – the kindness you showed to the children in your care and their families – but it is possible to choose to live by that kindness.'

Professor Hennessy goes on to say that this concept of a duty of care should again define us as we learn how to live in a post-pandemic world with such political, economic and social uncertainty. I wish for this to be the basis of a new social contract with government and, more widely, with our parliamentary democracy.

Hennessy says: 'The great question of UK politics ... is whether we can find the pessimism-breaking policies, the people, the purpose, the language, and the optimism to shift [our current] system and replace it with something much closer to who we are and, above all, who we can be' (Hennessy, 2022).

I believe it is within our gift to find the people, the purpose, the language and the optimism to shift our mental models, to see education as the building of who we can be.

I'd like to conclude the section with this thought: if we are to see education as the building of who we can be, we need to end the conflation in the policy discourse of social mobility and social justice. Social mobility is the lifting up of the few. Social justice is the lifting up of all. I believe education is (or should be) a force for social justice.

Building strong trusts

My thinking about the importance of organisational leadership (the first of the three domains) has developed over the years. In early 2022, CST published an influential discussion paper asking the question, 'What is a strong trust?' (Cruddas, 2022). Since then, we have engaged in a sector-wide discussion to understand how our proposed domains of organisational strength and resilience align with sector thinking and the emerging evidence base (Muijs, 2022).

Underpinning the original discussion paper was the concept of education as human flourishing. We need to think hard about how we create school environments where all children flourish. This means a relentless focus on high-quality, inclusive education – advancing education for all our children.

But we also need environments where the adults flourish. As Lynn Swaner and Andy Wolfe write: 'Where there are few flourishing adults, there will be few flourishing children' (Swaner and Wolfe, 2021).[2] So, we need to care deeply about our workforce and give renewed consideration to what 'good work' means and how we might strengthen our understanding of what it means to be a good employer.

And we need to think about the flourishing of our schools working together in deep and purposeful collaboration as one entity, under a single governance structure, to improve and maintain high educational standards across the trust. In my view, deep and purposeful collaboration is at the heart of the trust structure – it is the way we keep the focus on improvement at scale. And, from my point of view, structures are in fact very important because they create the conditions for this intensely focused collaboration.

We need to be explicit and eloquent about what constitutes a strong trust. CST's work on building strong trusts (Cruddas, 2023a) has seven domains:

1. Expert, ethical leadership.
2. High-quality, inclusive education.
3. School improvement at scale.
4. Strategic governance.
5. Workforce resilience and wellbeing.
6. Finance and operations.
7. Public benefit and civic duty.

---

2   The concept of flourishing draws on the thinking of Swaner and Wolfe, explored in a reflective review by Cruddas (2023b).

Part 1 of this book explores the first six domains. It examines the knowledge domains required to lead a trust. The seventh and final domain is the subject of Part 2.

Building strong and resilient organisations is key to education as human flourishing.

Knowledge building

I want to share a few thoughts about the importance of knowledge building. I have been very influenced in my thinking by Steve Rollett and Sir Ian Bauckham. Drawing on Legitimation Code Theory (Maton, 2014), Steve has written about the potential of trusts as knowledge-building institutions (Rollett, 2021). Sir Ian and I wrote a paper on knowledge building in 2021 (Bauckham and Cruddas, 2021). This paper offered four propositions, which are also a theory of change:

1. The goal is for every teacher in every classroom to be as good as they can be in what they teach (the curriculum) and how they teach (pedagogy).
2. For this to happen, we need to mobilise for every teacher the best evidence from research.
3. There is no [sustainable] improvement for pupils without improvement in teaching, and no improvement in teaching without the best professional development for teachers.
4. Strong structures (in groups of schools) can facilitate better professional development and thus better teaching and improvement for pupils.

This is not to dismiss the procedural processes of building capacity, undertaking a forensic analysis of need, supporting and deploying leadership, providing access to effective practice and monitoring improvements in the quality of provision. Indeed, these are essential. But without the intentional practice of knowledge building, improvement is not sustainable. It may not result in an enduring change in practice.

I believe this theory of change is still fundamentally important – it now forms part of a bigger conception of school improvement at scale in the work that Steve Rollett is leading (Rollett, 2024) and that is the subject of chapter two of this book.

Recurring themes

There are some themes that recur throughout the book, which it may be helpful to identify here.

Social justice and the common good

I wrote earlier in this Introduction that we need to end the conflation of social justice with social mobility. I feel very strongly about this. The principle of social justice is, I believe, closely connected to the conception of 'the common good'. Both of these concepts pertain to wider societal benefit over the more narrowly defined private good of individuals – although I think both are necessary.

Early conceptions of the common good were explored in Greek philosophy, notably by Aristotle. This is the idea that concepts like equity and justice can be achieved only through our sense of ourselves as citizens, through collective action, and active participation in the public realm and in public service.

Education is a good in itself but can also be mobilised both to create a more socially just society and a wider common good.[3] Within the trust sector, the charitable purpose of advancing education for public benefit points directly to this.

Relational trust

I recently read a book that has changed my thinking and perspective. I think I was grappling towards this, but Hilary Cottam in her book, *Radical Help: How We Can Remake the Relationships Between Us and Revolutionise the Welfare State* (Cottam, 2018), has had a profound impact on my thinking. She writes about six principles in remaking relationships:

1. *A vision of the good life (which is also the defining principle of our paper, A Good Life: Towards Greater Dignity for Learning Disabled People);*

2. *The need to develop capability, as opposed to manage need;*

3. *Relationships above all, over transactional cultures;*

4. *Connecting multiple forms of resource, rather than auditing money;*

5. *Creating possibility rather than containing risk; and*

6. *Taking care of everyone, as opposed to targeting individuals.*

Cottam (2018, p. 196)

---

3   The common good is also one of the most important principles of Catholic Social Teaching.

The shift towards relational engagement is one that I want to explore widely in this book. I believe it is the basis of a new social contract, not just with our colleagues in the organisations we lead but also with pupils and parents.

For the avoidance of doubt, I believe that we need rigour *and* relationships in our schools. Good, clear expectations around behaviour, for example, keep all children and adults safe. Most pupils in most lessons are well behaved, but poor behaviour is a major cause of stress for teachers, and impacts on our ability to retain our staff. It can also have a lasting impact on the outcomes of the pupils in the class. There is therefore a clear need for schools to have consistent and clear behaviour policies that promote positive behaviour in lessons and in school life. So, we need to be thorough and rigorous in ensuring our classrooms and schools are safe places. Also, we can enact more relational approaches.

I will return to this concept many times: the importance of relational trust as a leadership principle in its own right in chapter one; in our relationships with those who govern our organisations in chapter four; with those we lead (our colleagues) in chapter five; with other education and civic leaders in chapters seven and eight; and with the communities we serve in chapters six and nine.

Human flourishing

The final theme that I want to highlight here is human flourishing. I am going to return to Aristotelian thought and connect the common good, the good life and human flourishing. Cottam writes:

How should we live? This most basic of questions was asked by Aristotle, the philosopher to whom many of us return when our existing rules and systems no longer work. People need *meaning*, Aristotle argued, and they need *support* to grow and develop. Aristotle spoke of *eudaimonia*, which is often translated as happiness, but he was not in pursuit of an individual's elusive happiness. In fact, he argued that a rich, well-lived life would certainly contain periods of unhappiness, but to grow we need to aim for something big and we must risk disappointment. *Eudaimonia* is better translated as flourishing. And flourishing is a collective and political concept that embraces participation in the structures of society.

Cottam (2018, pp. 198–199, italics in original)

In CST's joint paper with the Church of England and Catholic Education Service (CST, Church of England Education Officer and Catholic Education Service, 2024), we see human flourishing as a collective vision for our education system. We believe our political leaders, schools and school leaders have a foundational question in common: how do children and young people, and those who educate them in our schools, flourish? We believe flourishing is both the optimal continuing development of children's potential (the substance of education) and living well as a human being.

In our joint paper we propose that this is a core purpose that is enacted in the dignity with which everyone is treated, the hope with which each is instilled, the relational community in which each is located and the practical wisdom with which each is taught.

We jointly believe that this is a vision centred on serving the common good, relentlessly prioritising the most vulnerable in every classroom, corridor, school and community. It is a vision that not only enables academic excellence but also makes long-lasting life-enhancing contributions to the flourishing of society through mutuality and solidarity, the pursuit of peace, the pursuit of social justice and prioritisation of the environment (see CST, Church of England Education Officer and Catholic Education Service, 2024).

These three themes of social justice and the common good, relational trust and human flourishing underpin each of the narratives of trust leadership, civic leadership and system leadership. They are a deep expression of what I believe.

A path through this book

This book is about leadership and I hope it speaks to leaders, particularly those who are leading school trusts. These are the stories from my perspective of learning from trust leaders, and seeing the system from the viewpoint of a national role. I have not led a school trust, but I am the founding chief executive of the organisation representing school trusts. So the book is an exploration and conceptual analysis of what I think we are learning as a system. It is also a sort or memoir of the last six years – less an academic exposition and more a series of reflections, drawing on promising practices within our sector.

Some of the chapters are not authored by me or are co-authored. Where CST has published a paper that I believe makes a huge contribution to the sector, I have edited and abridged it. This is the case for chapter two, which is authored by Steve Rollett, chapter three, which is an abridged version of Ben Newmark and Tom Rees's beautiful paper on five principles for inclusion, and chapter ten, which is an edited version of my paper with James Townsend and Ed Vainker on community anchoring.

I am using my original 2019 approach to the three nested leadership narratives, reconceptualised as the new domains of educational leadership, as the structure for this book.

1. The first part is about **trust leadership**, including how we build strong and resilient organisations. I will argue that school trusts create the conditions for deep collaborations among teachers and leaders to improve the quality of education.

2. The second part is about **civic leadership** – how we work with others to advance education as a wider common good. Civic trusts create the conditions for purposeful collaboration between and among trusts and other civic organisations.

3. The third part is about **system leadership**. Going further than previous conceptions of 'working beyond the school gate', the definition of system leadership used in this book is thinking about how we act *on*, rather than just acting *in* the system. System building goes beyond collaboration, and engages deliberate system design and system building.

I have tried to ensure that each chapter is self-contained so that you can pick up the book and read the chapter that speaks to you or seems most relevant to you at any point in time. But the book is also cumulative – the story of the different mindset and mental models we need to lead today as public leaders, in the world we live in rather than the world we might wish for.

I'll conclude this Introduction with this reflection: we need leaders who have the expertise, the professional will and professional generosity to contribute to system improvement as a form of system building. In this way, we will leverage leadership of the school system and enable the vastly more powerful and sustainable school system to be born.

References

Bauckham, I. and Cruddas, L. (2021). *Knowledge building: school improvement at scale*. CST. Available at: https://cstuk.org.uk/assets/pdfs/CST_Knowledge_Building_Whitepaper.pdf.

Cottam, H. (2018). *Radical Help: How We can Remake the Relationships Between us and Revolutionise the Welfare state*. Virago.

Cruddas, L. (2020). *Systems of meaning: three nested leadership narratives*. CST. Available at: https://cstuk.org.uk/knowledge/discussion-and-policy-papers/systems-of-meaning-three-nested-leadership-narratives-for-school-trusts/.

Cruddas, L. (2022). *What is a strong trust? A CST discussion paper*. CST. Available at: https://cstuk.org.uk/knowledge/guidance-and-policy/what-is-a-strong-trust-a-cst-discussion-paper/.

Cruddas, L. (2023a). *Building strong trusts*. CST. Available at: https://cstuk.org.uk/knowledge/guidance-and-policy/building-strong-trusts/.

Cruddas, L. (2023b). *Flourishing together – a reflective review*. CST. Available at: https://cstuk.org.uk/news-publications/cst-blogs/flourishing-together-a-reflective-review/.

Cruddas, L. (2023c). *The new domains of educational leadership*. CST. Available at: https://cstuk.org.uk/knowledge/thought-leadership/the-new-domains-of-educational-leadership/.

CST, Church of England Education Officer and Catholic Education Service (2024). *Flourishing together: a collective vision for the education system*. Available at: https://www.churchofengland.org/sites/default/files/2024-11/flourishing-together-a-collective-vision-for-the-education-system.pdf

Fullan, M. and Quinn, J. (2015). *Coherence: the Right Drivers in Action for Schools, Districts, and Systems*. Corwin.

Hennessy, P. (2022). *A Duty of Care: Britain Before and After Covid*. Penguin.

Maton, K. (2014). *Knowledge and Knowers: Towards a Realist Sociology of Education*. Routledge.

Muijs, D. (2022). *Trust quality: an overview of research*. CST. Available at: https://cstuk.org.uk/knowledge/guidance-and-policy/trust-quality-an-overview-of-research-policy/.

Rollett, S. (2021). *Communities of improvement: school trusts as fields of practice*. CST. Available at: https://cstuk.org.uk/assets/pdfs/ICE_10096_CST_School_Improvement_Whitepaper.pdf.

Rollett, S. (2024). *The DNA of trust-led school improvement: a conceptual model*. CST. Available at: https://cstuk.org.uk/knowledge/guidance-and-policy/the-dna-of-trust-led-school-improvement-a-conceptual-model/.

Swaner, L. and Wolfe, A. (2021). *Flourishing Together: a Christian Vision for Students, Educators, and Schools*. William B. Eerdmans Publishing.

PART 1
TRUST LEADERSHIP

Chapter 1:   Leading the organisation...31

Chapter 2:   Advancing education: the DNA of trust-led school
              improvement (by Steve Rollett) 44

Chapter 3:   Advancing education: five principles for inclusion
              (by Ben Newmark and Tom Rees) 67

Chapter 4:   Strategic governance...84

Chapter 5:   Operations and workforce 101

CHAPTER ONE
LEADING THE ORGANISATION

This first chapter, on leading the organisation, focuses on the importance of purpose, culture, ethics, relational trust, strategy and growth. It considers some of the literature from both within and outside our sector. Each of these themes could themselves be a book, so I do not pretend to offer a comprehensive review of the literature or an inclusive account of the topic. By definition, my writing is highly selective as I am drawing on literature and practice that I think may be helpful to trust leaders.

Purpose

Let's start with the core charitable 'object', or purpose, of most trusts in the country: to advance education for public benefit.[4] There is something wonderful that at the heart of the governing document for each trust (the articles of association) is also the moral purpose.

It feels important that this is not about 'providing' education – it is 'advancing' education. So this is something that requires action – to move our schools forward in a purposeful way, or to make progress. And perhaps even more importantly, the charitable object is not just for the benefit of those pupils in the organisations we lead, but for *public* benefit. At the heart of governance document, then, there is an imperative to look up and out. I'll write more about this later on in this book.

I said in the Introduction that I believe deep and purposeful collaboration is at the heart of the trust structure, and that this comes primarily from the power of purpose – the capacity to link people through a shared belief about the identify, meaning and mission of an organisation.

Viviane Robinson argues for the distinctiveness of the purposes of education. She says that only education has preparation as a major purpose: 'Preparation involves developing the distinctively human qualities and abilities such as reasoning, wisdom, and understanding, that enable people to manage their lives more intelligently and to appreciate the world in which they live' (Robinson, 2023, p. 10). She concludes that the proper function of education is to educate

---

4   As noted in the Introduction, the exception is Catholic trusts, where the charitable object is the advancement of the Catholic religion.

students in ways that achieve the three purposes of preparation, socialisation and autonomy (p. 11). This is perhaps what it means to advance education.

Most trusts interpret or translate their charitable purpose as mission or vision. Leadership theory tends to view mission and vision differently. For some, the mission describes the present activity of the organisation, while the vision paints a picture of the entity's future. For others, a mission expresses the organisation's core values and purpose.

We can get lost in the definitions and terminology. Dewar, Keller and Malhotra, in *CEO Excellence*, write:

It was somewhat disconcerting to find that the best CEOs used the terms vision, mission and company purpose as largely interchangeable. Communications and HR professionals, academics and we as consultants can argue all we want about the nuances of each term, but the fact remains that the best CEOs don't worry about such distractions – what matters for them is to have a clear and simply articulated North Star.

Dewar, Keller and Malhotra (2022, p. 29)

I find Simon Sinek's *Start with Why* (Sinek, 2009) offers a powerful way to lead with purpose. Sinek's visual representation involves three concentric circles, 'Why', 'How' and 'What'. The centre circle is 'Why', the next circle outwards is 'How', and finally, the outer circle is 'What'. Sinek believes that many organisations actually start with 'What' – they invert the concentric circles. His hypothesis is that those organisations that start with 'Why' are most successful. They are mission-led.

Dewar, Keller and Malhotra (2022) open their chapter on 'Vision practice – reframe the game' with a pivotal scene from the film *Invictus*, in which Nelson Mandela talks to Francois Pienaar about inspiring the South African rugby team ahead of the 1995 World Cup. What becomes clear in the course of that film (and indeed in the reality of the historical relationship between Mandela and Pienaar) is that the South African rugby team in 1995 were not just playing for a championship – they were playing to unite a nation torn apart by Apartheid. This resonates strongly for me.

So, a powerful way to think about leading with purpose in your trust is to start with 'Why'. Why does your trust exist? This is of course not something that the chief executive determines on their own – it is a collective vision that the board determines.

Culture

Leading with purpose around a collective 'why' is important, then. A trust's culture is equally important. The trust's culture must embody the behaviours, underlying mindsets and beliefs that shape how staff, students and other stakeholders work together. Culture cannot be left to accident or a vague statement of values posted on a website somewhere.

Viviane Robinson makes a compelling argument for why Enron failed. Enron was the energy, commodity and financial services company whose bankruptcy uncovered a financial scandal that also led to the downfall of other financial and auditing firms. Robinson writes: 'The corporate values that took pride of place in the company's annual reports were communication, respect, integrity and excellence. As subsequent events revealed, these values were hollow, for they provided no constraints whatsoever on the behaviour of its executives and employees' (Robinson, 2023, p. 82).

Interestingly, Robinson cites the work of Patrick Lencioni in her analysis of Enron, specifically his paper, 'Make your values mean something' (Lencioni, 2002). In Lencioni's book, *The Advantage* (2012), he poses six questions:

1. Why do we exist?
2. How do we behave?
3. What do we do?
4. How will we succeed?
5. What is most important right now?
6. Who must do what?

These six questions are a helpful framework for linking purpose (Why do we exist?) with culture (How do we behave?) and then translating this into strategy.

Dixons Academies Trust has perhaps done more than most on an approach to codifying culture. It uses Lencioni's framework – or at least the first four questions – to achieve clarity for everyone in the trust (set out in the box below). It explores all six critical questions on its open source platform (Dixons Academies Trust, 2024).

Dixons Academies Trust: who we are
Luke Sparkes, School Trust Leader of Dixons Academies Trust

Why do we exist?
Our mission is to challenge educational and social disadvantage in the North.

How do we behave?
Although our academies have the autonomy to choose their own vocabulary and nuance, all of them are built around the same three values and drivers that we all share.

As a highly professional team, together:

- we work hard on the things that matter, with humility
- we are good and kind
- we are motivated by mastery, autonomy and purpose.

What do we do?
Within our communities, we work together to establish joyful, rigorous, high-performing schools, which maximise attainment, value diversity, develop character and build cultural capital.

How will we succeed?
Talent first: people, more than strategy, create value – as all belong and grow together
Our talent is our most valuable resource, where nearly 80% of our budget is invested. We deploy our most vital people in roles where they can create significant value; we free our people from bureaucratic structures; and we afford our people the training and opportunities to expand their skills.

We see talent not as innate, but as unleashed, grown and developed. People have 'inherent growth tendencies', the drive to be better tomorrow than today. We believe that kind, helpful and honest feedback is a gift. As leaders we want our staff to be intrinsically motivated, cultivating self-determination through our three drivers: mastery, autonomy and purpose.

Academic rigour: with powerful knowledge, our students shape their own future
All children are entitled to a curriculum and to the powerful knowledge that maximises life chances. Children need powerful knowledge to understand and interpret the world: without it they remain dependent

upon those who have it. Our curriculum is designed to be remembered in detail, and is led by, collaborated on and delivered by high-quality subject specialists. The curriculum is the entitlement of all and we resist parental opt-outs.

Aligned autonomy: finding the optimal balance between consistency and self-determination

Our trust seeks the optimal balance between consistency and self-determination. We are aligned because we share the same mission and values, and because all Dixons students and staff should benefit from our best collective practice. But autonomy is also important because leadership and personal accountability are founded on ownership and self-direction, and because standardisation fails to respond to changing needs and fails to adapt to a changing environment.

'Doing the right work in the right way': virtues and ethics

I want to return to Viviane Robinson's work for a moment. In *Virtuous Educational Leadership*, she distinguishes between values and virtues. She says that 'virtues are desirable character traits evident in the thinking and action of persons. Philosophers disagree about whether values are qualities that are believed to worthy or qualities that are objectively worthy, whether or not they are believed to be so' (Robinson, 2023, p. 82).

Robinson attempts to integrate what she calls the generic knowledge needed to lead (strategic planning, budgeting, communication, problem-solving) with the educational domain-specific knowledge that enables effective leadership of educational organisations. She goes further than this and argues that we need a taxonomy of virtues for 'doing the right work in the right way'. For Robinson, the leader of an educational organisation must have:

- **Leadership virtues**: worthy leadership motivations.
- **Problem-solving virtues**: strategic, analytic and imaginative.
- **Interpersonal virtues**: integrity, respect, courage and empathy (Robinson, 2023, p. 95).

Robinson makes that case, then, that the leader, in the dedicated pursuit of educational purposes, develops the desirable qualities of character that enable them to do the *right* work in the *right* way.

I was part of a group of people and professional organisations in England who created the Framework for Ethical Leadership in Education (ASCL, 2019). The framework is based on both the UK's Seven Principles of Public Life (GOV. UK, 1995) and the set of virtues set out in the box below.

Trust – Leaders are trustworthy and reliable. We hold trust on behalf of children and should be beyond reproach. We are honest about our motivations.

Wisdom – Leaders use experience, knowledge and insight. We demonstrate moderation and self-awareness. We act calmly and rationally. We serve our schools and colleges with propriety and good sense.

Kindness – Leaders demonstrate respect, generosity of spirit, understanding and good temper. We give difficult messages humanely where conflict is unavoidable.

Justice – Leaders are fair and work for the good of all children. We seek to enable all young people to lead useful, happy and fulfilling lives.

Service – Leaders are conscientious and dutiful. We demonstrate humility and self-control, supporting the structures, conventions and rules that safeguard quality. Our actions protect high-quality education.

Courage – Leaders work courageously in the best interests of children and young people. We protect their safety and their right to a broad, effective and creative education. We hold one another to account courageously.

Optimism – Leaders are positive and encouraging. Despite difficulties and pressures, we are developing excellent education to change the world for the better.

More recently, I have begun to think that it is helpful to distinguish virtues (the desirable qualities of character in the leader) from professional ethics that *inhere in the work*. Professional ethics could be described as:

- protecting the children and people we serve
- upholding professional standards
- being accountable.

Of course, there is a big overlap between the desirable qualities of character in the leader and the way that leader and that organisation uphold professional ethics. The Principles of Public Life (as set out in the box below) are a helpful set of standards that enable trusts as organisations to uphold professional ethics.

Selflessness – The trust and its people should act solely in the interest of children and young people.

Integrity – The trust and its people must avoid placing themselves under any obligation to people or organisations that might try inappropriately to influence them in their work. Before acting and taking decisions, they must declare and resolve openly any perceived conflict of interest and relationships.

Objectivity – The trust and its people must act and take decisions impartially and fairly, using the best evidence and without discrimination or bias. Leaders should be dispassionate, exercising judgement and analysis for the good of children and young people.

Accountability – The trust and its people are accountable to the public for their decisions and actions and must submit themselves to the scrutiny necessary to ensure this.

Openness – The trust and its people should expect to act and take decisions in an open and transparent manner. Information should not be withheld from scrutiny unless there are clear and lawful reasons for so doing.

Honesty – The trust and its people should be truthful.

Leadership – The trust and its people should exhibit these principles in their own behaviour. They should actively promote and robustly support the principles and be willing to challenge poor behaviour wherever it occurs.

To lead an organisation well, we need both to pay attention to developing the desirable qualities of character in ourselves, and to consider ethical questions that inhere in the professional decisions we make every day.

The importance of relational trust in leadership

I listened spellbound to Professor Onora O'Neill's 2002 Reith Lectures contribution, *A question of trust* (O'Neill, 2002). I have been fascinated by this question ever since, particularly trust in public institutions. Much has been written in education literature about the importance of trust, notably recently Robinson's work on relational trust (Robinson, 2010), the rapid evidence assessment published by the Education Endowment Foundation (Nguyen et al., 2023) (more about this in chapter five), and Lemov and colleagues' *Reconnect* (Lemov et al., 2023).

Robinson defines leadership as using expert knowledge to solve complex problems, while building relational trust. She believes strongly that people do not want to work for leaders or organisations they don't trust.

But the need to build relational trust applies more widely than the people employed in our organisations. I'll keep returning to the importance of relational trust throughout this book.

In *Reconnect*, Lemov et al. talk about loss of faith in public institutions. They argue that this is a long-term trend that began in the twentieth century but has accelerated, with the public increasingly seeing institutions as 'incompetent' and 'ethically suspect' (Lemov et al., 2023, p. xxi). However, the authors are optimistic. In relation to children and young people, they argue that it is possible to combat this by helping students to feel a sense of belonging in their schools. They have some very specific proposals for how to do this, from 'rewiring the classroom' to send signals of belonging; wiring the school for socio-emotional learning and focusing on character education. Ultimately they are arguing for a wider view of the purpose of schooling, which is relational rather than simply transactional.

Lemov et al. also write about how to re-engage with parents and the community to create cultures of connection, meaning and belonging, thereby rebuilding trust and confidence in schools as public institutions. This is covered in greater detail in chapter nine of this book.

Early in 2024, I read a little treatise on *Trust in Public Life* edited by Claire Gilbert (2023), founder director of the Westminster Abbey Institute. In one of the essays in this collection, Anthony Ball offers four characteristics that should be advanced in order to improve the public's trust in institutions: honesty, humility, compassion and competence. He writes: 'If these are to be characteristics of institutions themselves then they also need to be features of behaviour of the public servants within the institutions' (Ball, 2023).

I agree with Ball that we need honesty, humility, compassion and competence in public life. However, I think we also need leaders who, as Anna Rowlands in the same essay collection says, have the power to illuminate darkness through the capacity to serve a wider public good, to struggle for justice in an unjust world, and to do so in such a way that the person does not grow harsh, *deepening* rather than losing their humanity in the course of struggle (Rowlands, 2023).

These are leaders who risk action, with others, towards building a common good.

Strategy

In his book *The Advantage*, Patrick Lencioni writes about 'smart' versus 'healthy' (Lencioni, 2012). He argues that smart organisations are good at the classic fundamentals of strategy, marketing, finance and technology, which he calls the 'decision sciences'. He believes this is only one half of the equation, and that being a healthy organisation is often neglected. This means minimal politics, minimal confusion, high morale, high productivity and low turnover.

Arguably, this chapter so far has focused on aspects of creating a healthy, ethical organisation with a strong purpose, built on relational trust. However, we do also need to give time to strategy. Developing a long-term strategy will support good decision-making in the short and medium term.

Traditional approaches to strategy invite us to consider trends, make an assessment of our strengths and weaknesses, consider the challenges and opportunities in the external environment, and then write down a set of priorities and actions that will determine what we do over the period of the strategy. The strategy is traditionally driven by a theory of change and supported by a methodology, which together explain how a set of interventions leads to educational improvement.

However, we live in a volatile and uncertain world. It is interconnected and fast paced, so Lang and Whittington argue that leaders have to develop strategies that take into account not only the long view but also the broad view:

The shift to a broad view of strategy has three key implications for leaders. First, it means they have to focus on anticipating contextual changes that might significantly and rapidly reshape the business environment, and it means they have to work with others to co-create value as they do that. Second, it means they have to imagine different time horizons and use them not just to make plans for the future but also to gain broader perspectives on the present. And third, it means they need to prepare themselves to rapidly adapt to changing circumstances, by constantly working on their agility and creating new options for themselves.

Lang and Whittington (2022)

In their book, *Strategy Beyond the Hockey Stick*, Bradley, Hirt and Smit invite us to move away from seeing strategy as an annual event and towards seeing strategy as a journey (Bradley, Hirt and Smit, 2018). The idea is that in the messy, fast-paced environment in which we work, the yearly planning cycle and linear world of annual plans are a poor fit for the dynamic reality of the world we inhabit. Which of our strategies survived the pandemic?

In this approach, the board determines the overall direction of travel over a two- to five-year period. This can be as brief as a series of three or four memorable statements, which can be sequential steps. Dixons Academies Trust's '2-to-5-year masterplan' is:

- Build greater structural, educational, financial and talent resilience to ensure consistently high standards across our trust.
- Expand our hubs in Leeds, Manchester and Liverpool (or in the North).
- Make our Centre for Growth the go-to place for our trust and the sector-lead for rigorous implementation; crafting school culture; and equality, diversity and inclusion.
- Provide education to 20,000 students across the North.

This plan is kept at the front and centre of strategy sessions. Importantly, it can be adjusted if the trust changes priorities, or to respond to external factors and trends.

Trust leaders then determine a series of 'big moves' that enact the strategy. They may focus on three to five big moves at any one time but will work through many more big moves over time to achieve their masterplan. Some big moves will be completed, paused or even scrapped, and others will emerge. In this way, the strategy process becomes a journey.

Dixons defines big moves as breakout opportunities that are 'hard to reverse'. Its current big moves are:

- business services transformation
- make transformation more programmatic – phase two implementation
- SEND (Dixons multi-disciplinary team)
- attendance
- joy.

This approach also ensures that the overall trust strategy is anchored in its context. It can be translated into outcomes and resource allocation.

There is no one right way to do strategy. However, the agility and clarity of strategy as a journey offers an innovative way of thinking about what Lencioni calls the 'decision science' of strategy.

Growth

As a subset of organisational strategy, most trusts have a 'growth strategy'. This is because around three-quarters of trusts in England (as of August 2024) comprise five schools or fewer. Growth is therefore a strategic imperative for many trusts if they are to build strong and sustainable organisations.

There are also other ways to consider growth. It could be through pupil numbers rather than numbers of schools. It could be different types of provision, such as resource bases or specialist and alternative provision.

However, it is worth pausing to consider that the pursuit of growth at all costs can be a distraction from core goals and values. As Alex Hill says in his book *Centennials*, 'Excellence can change the world. Growth on its own won't' (Hill, 2023).

So, a growth strategy that focuses only on the number of schools is unlikely in itself to result in excellence. Growth must be seen in the context of building institutional strength and resilience in the pursuit of educational excellence.

I'll return to the theme of growth in chapter five.

This chapter has considered some of the aspects of the leadership of an organisation. In the next chapter, we look specifically at the core business of school trusts – advancing education.

References

Association of School and College Leaders (ASCL) (2019). *Framework for ethical leadership in education.* Available at: https://ASCL/media/ASCL/Our%20view/Campaigns/Framework-for-Ethical-Leadership-in-Education.pdf.

Ball, A. (2023). 'Trust in institutions', in Gilbert, C. (ed.), *Trust in Public Life.* Haus Publishing.

Bradley, C., Hirt, M. and Smit, S. (2018). *Strategy Beyond the Hockey Stick.* McKinsey & Company.

Dewar, C., Keller, S. and Malhotra, V. (2022). *CEO Excellence: the Six Mindsets that Distinguish the Best Leaders from the Rest.* Nicholas Brealey Publishing.

Dixons Academies Trust (2024). *Our mission.* Available at: https://www.dixonsat.com/about/mission.

Gilbert, C. (ed.) (2023). *Trust in Public Life.* Haus Publishing.

GOV.UK (1995). *The seven principles of public life.* Available at: https://gov.uk/government/publications/the-7-principles-of-public-life/the-7-principles-of-public-life--2.

Hill, A. (2023). *Centennials: the 12 Habits of Great, Enduring Organisations.* Penguin.

Lang, T. and Whittington, R. (2022). 'The best strategies don't just take a long view. They take a broad view', *Harvard Business Review,* Strategy. Available at: https://hbr.org/2022/05/the-best-strategies-dont-just-take-a-long-view-they-take-a-broad-view.

Lemov, D., Lewis, H., Williams, D. and Frazier, D. (2023). *Reconnect: Building School culture for Meaning, Purpose and Belonging.* Jossey-Bass.

Lencioni, P. (2002). 'Make your values mean something', *Harvard Business Review,* 80(7), 113–117.

Lencioni, P. (2012). *The Advantage: Why Organisational Health Trumps Everything Else in Business.* Jossey-Bass.

Nguyen, D., Huat See, B., Brown, C. and Kokotsaki, D. (2023). *Reviewing the evidence base on school leadership, culture, climate and structure for teacher retention.* Education Endowment Foundation. Available at: https://d2tic4wvo1iusb.cloudfront.net/production/documents/projects/Review-of-leadership-approaches.pdf?v=1709411119.

O'Neill, O. (2002). *The Reith Lectures: Onora O'Neill – A question of trust* [radio broadcast]. BBC Radio 4. Available at: https://bbc.co.uk/programmes/p00ghvd8#:~:text=The%20Reith%20Lectures.%20The%20philosopher%20Onora.

Robinson, V. (2010). 'Instructional leadership to leadership capabilities: empirical findings and methodological challenges', *Leadership and Policy in Schools*, 9(1), 1–26.

Robinson, V. (2023). *Virtuous Educational Leadership: Doing the Right Work in the Right Way*. Corwin.

Rowlands, A. (2023). 'The roots of trust', in Gilbert, C. (ed.), *Trust in Public Life*. Haus Publishing.

Sinek, S. (2009). *Start with Why: How Great Leaders Inspire Everyone to Take Action*. Penguin.

CHAPTER TWO
ADVANCING EDUCATION: THE DNA OF TRUST-LED SCHOOL IMPROVEMENT

By Steve Rollett

Foreword by Leora Cruddas

In chapter one, I said that the core charitable 'object', or purpose, of most trusts in the country is to advance education for public benefit. I reflected that there is something wonderful that at the heart of the governing document is also the moral purpose. I offered a view that it is important that this is not about 'providing' education – it is 'advancing' education. So this is something that requires action – to move our schools forward in a purposeful way, or to make progress. This chapter explores these themes in greater depth.

The chapter is an abridged and edited version of the paper, 'The DNA of trust-led school improvement: a conceptual model' (Rollett, 2024). Like the paper, it is authored by Steve Rollett.

The DNA of trust-led school improvement

In 1953, two Cambridge scientists discovered the structure of DNA and declared they had 'discovered the secret of life'. Of course, although Crick and Watson's discovery was groundbreaking and laid the way for huge advances in scientific understanding, it was built on the work that had come before, including that by the X-ray crystallographer Rosalind Franklin. Theory, experiment and empirical evidence built over many years towards the understanding of DNA we now hold.

While knowledge develops and is legitimised by distinctive processes in different fields, the notion that knowledge often builds on knowledge, frequently in communities of practice, is important. While school trusts may not be grappling with uncovering the 'secret of life', they are in the vanguard of attempts to build knowledge about improvement in a group of schools. Just as Crick, Watson, Franklin and others contributed to the discovery of DNA, we are calling on the trust sector to work together to build knowledge about school improvement at scale. This is one reason why we are invoking the notion of discovery.

A second link we draw to the discovery of DNA is in the structure of the conceptual model we outline. Similar to how DNA is structured in a distinctive double helix shape, the conceptual model of trust-led school improvement is structured into three inseparable and intertwined strands forming a 'triple helix'. It is a theoretical device intended to illustrate the complex and interdependent considerations involved in school improvement.

We hope the conceptual model is useful to colleagues working in trusts, both to support their own school improvement practice and to work together across the sector to build knowledge about how to improve schools at scale.

Building strong trusts

One of the seven domains of 'Building strong trusts' (Cruddas, 2023) is 'school improvement at scale'. The paper argues that in strong trusts, 'A strong conception of quality and culture of continuous improvement is pervasive across all the schools in the group' (Cruddas, 2023, p. 3). Similarly, CST's description of a strong trust also highlights the fundamental importance of 'high quality, inclusive education'. Taken together, these two elements of CST's strong trust description recognise that a trust's fundamental objective is to improve education for the public benefit. As such, the other facets of the trust must be in service of the ongoing pursuit to enhance education of all children.

'Building strong trusts' laid down a mission for CST, and for the sector:

We are trying to codify how some of our best trusts do school improvement at scale – how they put improvement front and centre of all that they do; how they develop strong theorised models of improvement and then are able to implement/deliver these effectively across their schools. It is important to note that there is not a consensus around the model of improvement and there are different models of improvement which appear to be effective in different trusts and different contexts.

Cruddas (2023, p. 8)

This led to the establishment of CST's inquiry into trust-led school improvement in spring 2023. The work of that inquiry has helped to shape the approach and conceptual model described in this chapter.

The aim of this work is to establish a common set of concepts, language and framework that will allow trusts to explore, capture and compare their models of school improvement so that we can build more knowledge and a stronger evidence base about what is more likely to work when improving schools at scale.

School improvement at scale

The school trust sector is in the vanguard of school improvement in England. The first trusts were established primarily to improve schools where there had been long-term underperformance. Since then, as the trust sector has grown, it has been interwoven with the notion of school improvement.

Trust-led school improvement may be seen as a continuation and tightening up of previous collaborative, sector-led approaches, pioneered in London Challenge, the City Challenges and Teaching Schools. What is different in trusts is that these approaches are coupled with formal accountability in a single legal entity.

There is variability in the trust system, but we do know that some trusts have systemically improved schools in regions or nationally. The Department for Education's analysis demonstrates this success:

Robust analysis comparing annual cohorts of sponsored academies with similar local authority maintained schools shows that, on average, sponsored schools improve more quickly. Before they joined a trust, they performed significantly less well than otherwise similar schools. However, after joining a trust, the majority of sponsored academies demonstrate improvement, and their performance matches or exceeds these comparator schools. More than 7 out of 10 sponsored academies which were found to be underperforming as an LA maintained school in their previous inspection now have a good or outstanding rating.

Department for Education (2022)

Unfortunately, the empirical evidence base that explains *how* such improvements have been achieved is not yet sufficiently mature. In the meantime, the sector must work with the best knowledge it has about trust-led school improvement at scale. This will require a commitment to theory and system building as well as evidence collection. As Kurt Lewin famously noted, 'there is nothing so practical as a good theory'.

The conceptual model

The conceptual model is the output of CST's inquiry into trust-led school improvement, which was launched in 2023. The terminology of 'trust-led' is used to reflect the unique contribution this work is intended to make to the school improvement landscape, specifically focusing on what groups of schools in a single governance arrangement (a school trust) can do to improve education at scale. This is on the supposition there are affordances and possibilities a group of schools can leverage that a single school cannot. It should not be taken to imply a particular size, type of trust or the extent of 'central' control exerted within a trust.

The conceptual model is structured as three strands:

1. **Curate clear goals:** This strand is about defining clear purposes, strategies and goals so you know what you're aiming for and how you how you plan to get there.

2. **Build capability and capacity:** This strand is about shaping the people, culture and capacity within the organisation, in order to create the conditions for sustainable improvement.

3. **Implement improvement initiatives:** This strand is about the ongoing process of implementing improvement, iterating and refining as plans are enacted.

Three Trust-led school improvement strands & their components

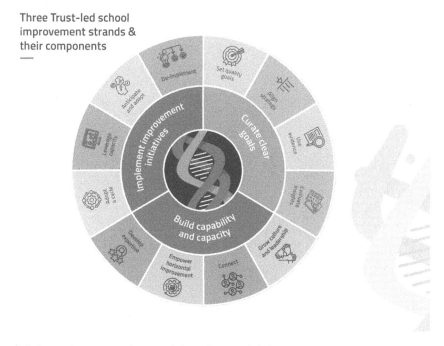

It is important to understand that the model does not seek to specify what a trust might want to improve within its schools, but rather it outlines the key aspects of how a school improvement process, strategy or model is enacted

within the trust. Accordingly, it does not assert that particular aspects of school practice, such as curriculum, pedagogy and behaviour, should be improved (though a trust might determine they should be).

This allows the model to 'speak to' improvement models and strategies that span the potentially infinite range of things a school or trust could seek to improve. If a trust thinks the curriculum, for example, is central to school improvement, then this would be reflected in various components within the model, including how the trust defines its conception of quality and improvement goals. It could also flow into other aspects of the model. For example, there might be considerations linked to school culture that are pertinent to curriculum improvement, or the development of expertise.

The model in more detail

Essentially, the model is intended to help trusts trace a pathway from what their improvement model/strategy intends to address to a holistic consideration of how they do this.

Curate clear goals

Define clear purposes, strategies and goals so you know what you're aiming for and how you intend to get there

COMPONENT	IN MORE DETAIL	EXAMPLES OF THIS IN PRACTICE
Set quality goals	Define the quality the trust is aiming for and the specific goals needed to achieve this.	• What the school improvement model/ strategy says (explicitly or implicitly) is effective practice. • Codifying what effective practice looks like in schools and classrooms. • What the school articulates, for example through job descriptions or a school prospectus, about its aims.
Allign strategy	Ensure alignment between school improvement objectives and wider trust strategy.	• Embedding wider trust improvement objectives into school level improvement plans. • Having a clear strategy for what is determined as a trust and where improvement planning sits locally and why. • Having clear and coherent improvement goals and strategies that are understood by all.
Use evidence	Use evidence to identify the actions most likely to build momentum in the desired direction.	• Building evidence into improvement models and strategies. • Staff research reading groups. • Evidence/research libraries staff can use.
Evaluate insights	Use quality evaluative tools to understand the performance of schools and the trust.	• Using trust peer review to identify strengths and areas for improvement. • Using a common assessment system for reading at Year 7, to allow comparisons across the group. • Using a trust-wide data system to provide insight on where performance is stronger/weaker to inform strategy and deployment.

Build capability and capacity

Shaping the people, culture and capacity within the organisation to create the conditions for sustainable improvement

COMPONENT	IN MORE DETAIL	EXAMPLES OF THIS IN PRACTICE
Develop expertise	Put expertise and professional learning at the heart of improvement.	• Prioritising CPD within improvement plans. • Encouraging teachers to be part of subject communities. • Investing in high quality leadership development programmes for new leaders.
Empower horizontal improvement	Improve practice across a group of schools simultaneously, rather than just 'one school at a time'.	• Trust-wide subject networks and CPD. • Setting shared improvement priorities across the trust. • Bringing together subject leaders across the trust to develop and/or align the curriculum.
Connect	Build connections across the organisation.	• Ensure staff don't work in silos by establishing working groups on specific issues. • Holding whole-trust conferences to support improvement. • Participating in professional networks and initiatives beyond the school/trust.
Grow culture and leadership	Establish a culture where leadership and teaching can flourish.	• Being explicit about 'how we do it here' (whether at trust or school level). • Consciously curating the leadership behaviours that are valued through mentoring and coaching. • Codifying what standards of classroom behaviour explicitly teaching these to children

Implement improvement initiatives

The ongoing process of implementing improvement, iterating and refining as plans are enacted

COMPONENT	IN MORE DETAIL	EXAMPLES OF THIS IN PRACTICE
Adopt a cycle	Adopt the behaviours that drive implementation (Engage, Unite, Reflect), Do this whilst tending to contextual factors but flexible implementation process: Explore, Prepare, Deliver, Sustain	• Embedding EEF Implementation guidance in improvement initiatives. • Establishing an improvement cycle that allows for evaluation. • Providing time for staff to reflect on practice.
Leverage capacity	Match improvement initiatives with capacity to deliver.	• Deploying expert teachers from a central team to support subject teaching. • Deploying into a school leaders who have prior experience of 'turn around' in the trust. • A budget to support improvement initiatives across the trust.
Anticipate and adapt	Know what's likely to cause failure and how you will spot it. Learning from it and adapting or ejecting the failing action.	• Drawing on experience to anticipate likely implementation challenges. • Evaluating and adapting curriculum plans. • Establishing key metrics and milestones that will indicate the path to success.
De-implement	De-implement initiatives that are not effective, or less effective than alternative options.	• Reviewing the opportunity cost of low-impact teaching initiatives. • Reducing teacher workload. • Having a 'one in, one out' policy when introducing new initiatives. What will we stop doing in order to implement this?

A common conversation

While there is some research into the efficacy of trusts as school improvers (Hutchings and Francis, 2018), there is not yet sufficient research into *how* the most effective trusts are improving schools systemically. Indeed, in 2018, Hutchings and Francis argued

There is little evidence that ... the considerable knowledge base about how to improve struggling schools is being effectively passed. ... We repeat our call for further analysis and learning from successful [trusts] (and other successful groups of schools), and for opportunities to be created for school groups to learn from each other.

Hutchings and Francis (2018, p. 4)

This reflection refers to one aspect of school improvement: 'struggling' schools. But the imperative of improvement is not the preserve of the weakest schools; it is something that all schools strive for. However, it is plausible that how a trust nurtures improvement in a school that is already providing a good quality for its pupils might be different to how it leads improvement in a school that is in need of significant turnaround.

This is reflected in Carter and McInerney's 'four phases of a school improvement journey' (Carter and McInerney, 2020). Added to this we can also hypothesise that variances in school and trust context add further complexity, and there will undoubtedly be other factors too.

There is also a linguistic and conceptual hurdle to overcome in the sector. The notion of the 'school improvement model' is one that many trusts seem to recognise, and some talk about, but its meaning seems to vary. In some trusts it's about the staffing structure, while in others it's about specific curriculum and pedagogical approaches. Others prefer to talk about a strategy rather than a model, and sometimes these are used interchangeably.

In part, this lack of common vocabulary may be because trust leaders appear to think in different ways about how to bring about school improvement, but it also seems to be because the terminology itself lacks an agreed definition.

As a result of the above, it is not yet possible to identify and codify a single evidence-based and highly specified 'school improvement model' or strategy that trusts should follow. Indeed, it may be that due to the complexity involved, it will never be possible – or desirable – to land on a single model, strategy or process; a one size that fits all.

While the evidence about specific trust models of improvement is underdeveloped, there is an abundant literature and evidence base about improvement processes more generally, from industry as well as public services. Starting from these, it is possible to construct an optimal conceptual model that captures what are considered to be the most common facets of effective improvement practices.

School improvement processes, models and approaches

The school improvement cycle has historically tended to involve auditing current performance, developing strategic plans and interventions, implementing changes and monitoring/reviewing progress. While logical, some suggest such models oversimplify improvement into a linear sequence rather than continuous learning (Maden, 2001).

Other research focuses on specific activities likely to improve schools, rather than an overarching process. Common factors cited include quality teaching, monitoring progress, and high expectations (Muijs et al., 2004). However, critics argue that lists of decontextualised factors insufficiently capture the complexity of improvement (Harris, Jones and Baba, 2013).

Park and colleagues propose an ecological model, recognising school improvement as an open, interactive, non-linear process involving adaption to changing contexts (Park, Daly and Guerra, 2013). Harris emphasises the importance of capacity building across the organisation, not isolated initiatives. As such, sustained learning is seen to be key to improvement (Harris, Jones and Baba, 2013).

Barker and Rees use the term 'persistent problems' as the purpose for school leaders' (and indeed improvement) work (Barker and Rees, 2019). They draw on the work of Mary Kennedy. In her 2016 paper, 'Parsing the practice of teaching', Kennedy represents teaching through five 'persistent problems', using this term to represent an understanding of not just the behaviours or moves that teachers carry out, but the purpose behind these (Kennedy, 2016). Barker and Rees develop this into an approach to the work of school leaders. Their seven persistent problems are:

1. setting direction and building alignment
2. enlisting staff contribution and ensuring staff development
3. organising and staffing the curriculum
4. attending to pupil behaviour and wider circumstances

5. diagnosing, prioritising and managing resources effectively to build and implement strategy

6. managing an efficient and effective organisation/administration

7. developing personal expertise, self-regulation and resilience.

Barker and Rees draw on the school improvement literature to make some strong 'bets' on particular areas that are important in relation to school improvement.

Insights from improvement processes in healthcare

Recent trends in the healthcare sector show quality and improvement models are increasingly focusing more on people. Vanhaecht et al. argue, 'High quality is only possible if we include core values of dignity and respect, holistic care, partnership, and kindness with compassion in our daily practice for every stakeholder at every managerial and policy level' (Vanhaecht et al., 2021).

Furthermore, practice in the health sector situates quality improvement alongside three other aspects of quality management: quality planning, quality control and quality assurance (Shah, 2020).

Quality improvement is a systematic and applied approach to solving a complex issue, through testing and learning, measuring as you go, and deeply involving those closest to the issue in the improvement process. Anyone who has undertaken quality improvement work will testify that it is not easy – you are generally tackling a problem to which we do not know the solution, and where part of the answer is about behaviours, and hearts and minds.

Shah (2020)

Similarly, Claessens and colleagues situate quality improvement within a broader framework of quality management, which includes quality design and planning, quality control, quality leadership, quality culture and quality context (Claessens et al., 2022).

On the issues of culture for improvement, the Virginia Mason Partnership identified six key drivers for a culture of continuous improvements that emphasises aspects such as cultural readiness, relationships and the importance of embedding improvement routines into everyday practice (Burgess, 2022).

Implementing improvement

The process of improving schools reaches beyond just the enactment of specific initiatives. This is why the conceptual model we outline encompasses a broad view of improvement that takes account of a range of phenomena that are likely to underlie improvement processes in a trust, including objective setting, building culture and connecting colleagues across the organisation.

That said, somewhere within a trust or school's approach to improvement there are likely to be specific initiatives intended to improve particular aspects of education. Implementing these initiatives well is at least as important as the process of identifying the things you want to improve and understanding the associated evidence.

The Education Endowment Foundation (EEF) has updated guidance on implementation (Sharples, Eaton and Boughelaf, 2024). This is a useful reference point. It also takes a broad view of implementing improvement, emphasising the social aspect of effective improvement. It is a slightly different proposition to the conceptual model we have outlined because our work is intended to speak to trust-led school improvement, and the affordances that may bring, rather than school improvement more generally. But the EEF guidance reflects some similar concepts and is a useful framework to support the implementation of evidence-informed decisions.

The EEF's three recommendations on effective implementation in schools are listed in the following table.

1. Adopt the behaviours that drive effective implementation
• Engage people so they can shape what happens while also providing overall direction. • Unite people around what is being implemented, how it will be implemented, and why it matters. • Reflect, monitor, and adapt to improve implementation.
2. Attend to the contextual factors that influence implementation
• Consider whether an approach is evidence-informed, suitable for the setting and feasible to implement. At the same time, leaders should develop an infrastructure that supports implementation, and ensure that the right people are in place who can lead and influence implementation.
3. Use a structured but flexible implementation process
• Treat implementation as an ongoing process of learning and reflection throughout the Explore, Prepare, Deliver and Sustain phases of the effort. Use a range of implementation strategies (not training alone) to support changes in practice.

By attending to the contextual factors, and engaging, uniting and reflecting throughout an ongoing process of continuous learning and improvement, an organisation improves implementation and the way in which the process of change is experienced by staff. This in turn fosters a positive implementation climate, which further supports effective implementation (i.e. is self-reinforcing).

We reflect such ideas in the 'Implementing Improvement' part of our conceptual model, but it is important to note EEF's framework is broader than the 'doing' phase alone, and you will see helpful overlap between the EEF's guidance and several other components of our conceptual model for trust-led school improvement.

The vertical, horizontal and systemic

Traditionally, school improvement has been concerned with what can be achieved within and by the unit of the school, over a specified period of time (thereby establishing two dimensions of improvement). This has tended to lead to a model of trust-led school improvement that deals with each school separately, plotting each school's path on an improvement trajectory distinct from the others. In some cases, this has meant trusts addressing improvement challenges in their schools sequentially or in isolation. This is not necessarily poor practice by the trust, and many trusts and schools will have benefited from the use of such an approach.

However, what if there is untapped potential in looking at a third dimension – improvement across the trust – and a fourth dimension – improvement across the sector? This is not a question about control from the centre, rather it is about creating a space to consider how a trust can facilitate and enable collective capacity and expertise from across the group, leveraged to maximum effect for all pupils, in every school, first within the trust and ultimately across the sector beyond it.

If we characterise the traditional segmented approach to school improvement as being vertical in nature (an upward path of improvement for each school in isolation), acknowledging the role of the trust brings another dimension into play: the horizontal. This is the plane that cuts across schools and internal trust boundaries, allowing us to plan and implement improvements that leverage the collective capacity of the trust.

This is where recent theorisation about trusts as knowledge-building institutions comes into play as a key lever for improvement (Bauckham and Cruddas, 2021). It is also the perspective that informs growing efforts in the sector to establish communities of improvement across trusts (Rollett, 2021) and to bring together professional development in new and powerful ways across the group (Barker and Patten, 2022). All of these approaches to improvement are situated in the 'horizontal plane': trust-wide improvement.

This allows us to consider and plan for improvement activity that works in both dimensions: within individual schools (vertical), or across all schools within a trust (horizontal). It brings into sharper focus the additional value of trusts that may not be acquired through the use of external school improvement services or input from third-party organisations: collective capacity and efficacy across the group.

As the sector matures, a further question arises about how to harness the collective capacity of trusts across the system. If we want to improve the life chances of all children, then we need to reduce disparities in performance between trusts as well as within them.

Navigating complexity

The conceptual model is not a manual that specifies in detail how all trusts should go about improving their schools – it is an overarching framework. Schools and trusts are adaptive complex systems and it is hard 'to predict how social complex adaptive systems such as schools react to change' (Keshavarz et al., 2010, p. 1473). This suggests that approaches to trust-led school improvement are unlikely to be successful if it is assumed that mechanistic improvement models can simply be replicated from one trust to another.

This is also reflected in Mason's argument that educational improvement is not only highly contextual but also contingent on a complex range of interrelated dependencies (Mason, 2008). As such,

change in education, at whatever level, is not so much a consequence of effecting change in one particular factor or variable, no matter how powerful the influence of that factor. It is more a case of generating momentum in a new direction by attention to as many factors as possible.

Mason (2008, p. 44)

While it is hard to predict cause-and-effect relationships at the level of whole-school effectiveness, we know more about cause-and-effect relationships at the more granular levels of teacher and leader practice. Therefore, leaders should particularly attend to these because – taken together – a multi-pronged improvement programme consisting of actions known to yield impact is our best bet to navigate a complex system:

Despite complexity theory's relative inability to predict the direction or nature of change, by implementing at each constituent level changes whose outcome we can predict with reasonable confidence, we are at least influencing change in the appropriate direction and surely stand a good chance of effecting the desired changes across the complex system as a whole.

Mason (2008, p. 46)

Illustrations of the conceptual model

I want to provide three case studies illustrating the conceptual model. The first is from Northern Education Trust on a reading strategy to improve pupils' literacy so that all pupils can access the GCSE curriculum. The second is Danes Educational Trust on developing oracy. The third is from Dixons Academies Trust on decolonising the curriculum.

Northern Education Trust (NET): reading
Links to the conceptual model

- Curate clear goals: set quality goals, align strategy.
- Build capability and capacity: develop expertise, empower horizontal improvement.
- Implement improvement initiatives: leverage capacity.

NET recognises the centrality of reading in education. A reading-strategies overview document discusses the importance of literacy and reading in improving outcomes and the life chances of our students. The definition of quality in literacy and reading, however, is multifaceted. NET's literacy strategy is divided into three strands: the mechanics of reading, reading for leisure and pleasure, and reading for knowledge. Within these three strands, there are 47 systems in place to improve reading in NET schools. All systems were created by NET school leaders and have been adopted by all secondaries in the trust.

Mechanics of reading

The trust tests the reading ages of pupils from Year 7 onwards. For those children whose reading ages are furthest from their chronological ages – for example, 18 months younger – it then implements a phonics-based intervention.

The aim of the NET intervention is to provide that missing phonics support. These pupils are taken out of their lessons for 30 to 40 minutes a day, in order to do intense, phonics-based reading practice in small groups. The aim is that, by the time they reach Year 10, their reading level is high enough to access the GCSE curriculum.

During a visit to a NET school, an Ofsted inspector questioned the value of a scheme that involves taking children out of class for 30 to 40 minutes each day for six weeks. The trust's response was that these pupils were unable to access the curriculum, anyway – and would continue to be unable to access it for the next four years without this intervention. This was accepted by the inspector.

Reading for leisure and pleasure

a. Reading routes

Every NET secondary has a map on its wall that looks like a giant London tube map. Each map features landmarks of its local area, including NET academies.

So, for example, schools around Newcastle have a map that features the Millennium Bridge and the Angel of the North; the map for Middlesbrough schools features the Middlesbrough Institute of Modern Art.

The stations, however, are not local areas – they're books. Each line represents a genre of book – there are 18 lines in total, including thrillers, classics, dystopian fiction and adventure novels – and has six stops, or books, along its route.

During the first half of the autumn term, all Year 7 pupils at a NET school attend an assembly where the teacher gives them a brief synopsis of each book on one of the tube lines. The children are given a sheet of paper with the names of all six books on that line; they tick the one they want, and that afternoon the teacher delivers their chosen book to them. As they progress through the school, they also work their way through different tube lines.

When pupils have read 50 books from the map, they are rewarded with an Amazon Kindle.

b. Drop Everything and Read

One afternoon each week, schools have a 'Drop Everything and Read' afternoon. First, form tutors read to their classes; afterwards, pupils have a guided-reading session with their chosen book.

Reading for knowledge

a. Read Through Me

Children who are read aloud to frequently by adults are much more likely to achieve reading fluency. The 'Read Through Me' strategy therefore provides pupils with the opportunity to hear teachers read aloud to them on a regular basis.

NET teachers are trained to read aloud in a way that demonstrates their thought processes as they read. So, for example, an English teacher might read from a set text, stopping along the way to say: 'I'm going to pause here, because there's an ellipsis in the text, and I'm thinking about what's going to happen next.'

Pupils who are not fluent readers will not automatically make the connection between the punctuation marks they see on the page and the way the text should be read. So teachers make that link explicit as they read.

'Read Through Me' is not, however, limited to English or arts subjects – it is used across the curriculum. So a business studies teacher might look at a case study with pupils; reading aloud the subtitle and logo gives pupils most of the information they need about the business in question.

Similarly, in maths, teachers will read aloud exam questions to the class, drawing attention to key words: 'I know I'm being asked to calculate something here', or 'I need to multiply something.'

They will also explain more complicated words – 'equilateral', for example, or 'rhombus' – as they encounter them. This strategy, the trust states, 'allows students to view reading as an active process and provides opportunities for precise vocabulary instruction'.

b. Word Anatomy

A recent GCSE maths question featured the word 'apartment', which was unfamiliar to many pupils. They would refer to living in a flat. The 'Word Anatomy' strategy, therefore, teaches the students the method of decoding unfamiliar vocabulary and allows them to make links to other vocabulary across the curriculum. It does this using morphology, which is the process of breaking down words into their constituent parts.

This is not an exhaustive illustration of the entire NET approach, but gives an overview of the different strands and approaches.

Danes Educational Trust: developing oracy

Links to the conceptual model

- Use evidence: use evidence to identify the actions most likely to build momentum in the desired direction.
- Evaluate insights: Use quality evaluative tools to understand the performance of schools and the trust.

The role of a trust and its schools is to provide children with a good education and good GCSE and A-level results. But can it offer them anything more?

Dr Valentine, the trust's chief executive, visited schools with a long history of offering outstanding education, looking to find out what they were offering that no one else was. Long before it became a buzzword in education, it was clear that these schools were teaching their students oracy. Regardless of background and academic ability, the students at these schools were confident, articulate and at ease with the spoken word.

In order to replicate this verbal confidence at Danes, the trust seconded a number of teachers from across its schools to lead an oracy evaluation. One teacher in particular had done quite a lot of oracy work previously; she therefore began training oracy leads in each of the trust's schools.

The trust held a number of oracy forums, bringing teachers together to discuss the work.

The student leadership from the trust's schools were also brought into the project. The Danes Learner Voice Council was launched, with more than 60 students from the trust's secondary schools. Each student was tasked with conducting an investigation, exploring which elements of teaching and learning were having the greatest impact on their education. They explored the issue with staff and fellow students, and then reported back to the trust central forum, including the chief executive.

The evaluation of the Learner Voice Council project revealed that students' understanding of teaching and learning had improved by 83% from the baseline. Their oracy had improved by 50% and their presentational skills by 76%.

Students' wellbeing, self-esteem, self-confidence and teacher relationships had also either increased or hugely increased. And the facilitating members of staff also expressed satisfaction. One said:

'It has been a high point in my career. ... Could not think of a better initiative for a school to run.'

The Learner Voice Council project was subsequently rolled out to Danes' primary schools too. Primary students undergo a structured four-stage process, planning, auditing, implementing and evaluating a chosen aspect of school life – for example, at one primary, they focused on enhancing the classroom to ensure that it catered to all students, regardless of need.

At primary level, students showed increased scores in 15 of the 17 impact measures, between baseline and final data collection. Their scores on measures related to self-efficacy increased by between 4.22% and 11.59%.

Oracy is now a key element of all schools in the trust – so much so that it no longer needs to be led from the centre. A visitor to any Danes primary classroom will immediately be greeted by the two classroom ambassadors: 'Welcome to our classroom,' they say. 'Today, we are learning about these topics ...'.

The classroom ambassador roles rotate on a regular basis, so everyone has a turn. The day's ambassadors wear lanyards, so that they are easily identifiable to their classmates and to visitors. The welcome is now so engrained a part of classroom life that it no longer feels like a performance – instead, it is simply how one greets a visitor.

'Many jobs will be taken by AI in the future,' says Dr Valentine, 'so people will want employees who are warm, who are articulate and who have high emotional intelligence. That's part of our DNA here.'

Dixons Academies Trust: decolonisation of the curriculum
Links to the conceptual model

- Curate clear goals: set quality goals, align strategy.
- Build capability and capacity: develop expertise, empower horizontal improvement.
- Implement improvement initiatives: leverage capacity.

Funmilola Stewart and the Equality, Diversity and Inclusion Strategy Team at Dixons Academies Trust have developed a process for decolonisation of the curriculum. This is how they conceptualise it.

Funmilola is also the co-author of CST's paper on 'Powerful knowledge as social justice' (Stewart and Thompson, 2021).

The largest cohort of Team Dixons is our children. If we are truly committed to equality, diversity and inclusion, they must be able to see it, understand it and feel it. This means that stronger and more robust than any policy is our curriculum. The time we spend with our children is primarily in our classrooms delivering instruction; as such, our curricula must give life to our equality, diversity and inclusion thinking. For our curricula to achieve this, equality, diversity and inclusion must be pervasive, informing every decision taken in our classrooms. This means that we are beholden to ensure it is central to our professional growth offer.

If our teaching staff know and live our equality, diversity and inclusion values, they will be able to iterate this in their teaching, the accountability to do so will be clear and the benefits tangible to all.

This begins with an appreciation that our trust will have to think more completely and more appreciatively than is expected in society. We must accept that this will be complicated and have consequence.

If we truly start from the most vulnerable in our development of curricula and academy-culture, we cannot select the vulnerabilities society (or we) find palatable. There are nine protected characteristics, in our thinking, each must be treated with equity.

The nine protected characteristics are legally protected both by, and from, society. Again, this means that, for many of our staff and students, the likelihood of experiencing behaviours or treatment from which they require protection is ever present.

Where society is tacitly accepting, or indeed endorsing, of behaviours, Dixons will not be. This is a high bar to hold – justly and necessarily high.

Our staff and students will not face discrimination, will not discriminate against others and our curricula will actively protect these characteristics. This demands a huge effort, investment and commitment that society would be fundamentally comfortable for us to ignore.

As this is a path-finding and sector-leading initiative, our lead schools must be in the vanguard. Our lead schools must own this work and embrace it wholly.

Set quality goals

- By 2025, Dixons' national voice will be sector-leading on equality, diversity and inclusion.
- By 2023, all cross cutting team leads will be trained to expertise on equality, diversity and inclusion.
- BAME (Black, Asian and minority ethnic) students will report feeling represented in the curriculum equitably to white students.

Align strategy

Dixons 2-to-5-year masterplan includes making the Centre for Growth the go-to place for our trust and the sector-lead for rigorous implementation; crafting school culture; and equality, diversity and inclusion.

Develop expertise and empower horizontal improvement

- Appointed (in 2022) as a trust assistant principal for anti-racism to lead the cross cutting team to embed the decolonisation of the curriculum.
- Trained the trust assistant principals to be domain experts in equality, diversity and inclusion in order to centre this thinking in all curricular decisions (in 2023).
- Ensured mechanisms are in place to capture the intentional equality, diversity and inclusion of our curricula and feedback (2023).
- Captured staff and student feedback on the representation of our equality, diversity and inclusion curricula (2023).
- Share our equality, diversity and inclusion curricular work across our sector (2024).

Into the future

Research suggests improvement in complex organisations is not a linear activity, so a vital part of the process is ongoing learning and iteration. For this reason, the three strands of the model should be thought of as feedback loops rather than work streams to be completed. Although displayed as separate parts for reasons of clarity, the reality is that the strands are intertwined. We hope this proves useful in supporting trusts to think about and refine their own improvement models and strategies, helping to make the implicit become explicit.

References

Barker, J. and Patten, K. (2022). *Professional development in school trusts: capacity, conditions and culture.* CST. Available at: https://cstuk.org.uk/knowledge/guidance-and-policy/development-in-school-trusts-capacity-conditions-and-culture/.

Barker, J. and Rees, T. (2019). *Persistent problems: finding the purpose for expert school leadership.* Ambition Institute. Available at: https://www.ambition.org.uk/blog/persistent-problems-expert-school-leadership.

Bauckham, I. and Cruddas, L. (2021). *Knowledge building: school improvement at scale.* CST. Available at: https://cstuk.org.uk/assets/pdfs/CST_Knowledge_Building_Whitepaper.pdf.

Burgess, N. (2022). *Six key lessons from the NHS and Virginia Mason Institute partnership.* Available at: https://www.wbs.ac.uk/news/six-key-lessons-from-the-nhs-and-the-virginia-mason-institute-partnership/.

Carter, D. and McInerney, L. (2020). *Leading Academy Trusts.* John Catt.

Claessens, F., Seys, D., Brouwers, J., Van Wilder, A., Jans, A., Castro, E.M. *et al.* (2022). 'A co-creation roadmap towards sustainable quality of care: a multi-method study', *PLoS ONE*, 17(6).

Cruddas, L. (2023). *Building strong trusts.* CST. Available at: https://cstuk.org.uk/knowledge/guidance-and-policy/building-strong-trusts/.

Department for Education (2022). *The case for a fully trust-led system.* HM Government. Available at: https://assets.publishing.service.gov.uk/media/62865295d3bf7f1f433ae170/The_case_for_a_fully_trust-led_system.pdf.

Harris, A., Jones, M. and Baba, S. (2013). 'Distributed leadership and digital collaborative learning: a synergistic relationship?', *British Journal of Educational Technology*, 44(6), 926–939.

Hutchings, M. and Francis, B. (2018). *Chain Effects 2018: the impact of academy chains on low-income pupils.* The Sutton Trust. Available at: https://www.suttontrust.com/wp-content/uploads/2019/12/Chain-Effects-2018.pdf.

Kennedy, M. (2016). 'Parsing the practice of teaching', *Journal of Teacher Education*, 67(1), 6–17.

Keshavarz, N., Nutbeam, D., Rowling, L. and Khavarpour, F. (2010). 'Schools as social complex adaptive systems: a new way to understand the challenges of introducing the health promoting schools concept', *Social Science and Medicine*, 70(10), 1467–1474.

Maden, M. (ed.) (2001). *Success Against the Odds, Five Years On: Revisiting Effective Schools In Disadvantaged Areas*. Routledge.

Mason, M. (2008). 'What is complexity theory and what are its implications for educational change?', *Educational Philosophy and Theory*, 40(1), 35–49.

Muijs, D., Harris, A., Chapman, C., Stoll, L. and Russ, J. (2004). 'Improving schools in socioeconomically disadvantaged areas: a review of research evidence', *School Effectiveness and School Improvement*, 15(2), 149–175.

Park, V., Daly, A.J. and Guerra, A.W. (2013). 'Strategic framing: how leaders craft the meaning of data to maximize strategic change', *Educational Policy*, 27(1), 123–149.

Rollett, S. (2021). *Communities of improvement: school trusts as fields of practice*. CST. Available at: https://cstuk.org.uk/knowledge/thought-leadership/communities-of-improvement-school-trusts-as-fields-of-practice/.

Rollett, S. (2024). *The DNA of trust-led school improvement: a conceptual model*. CST. Available at: https://cstuk.org.uk/knowledge/guidance-and-policy/the-dna-of-trust-led-school-improvement-a-conceptual-model/.

Shah, A. (2020). 'How to move beyond quality improvement projects', *British Medical Journal*, 370.

Sharples, J., Eaton, J. and Boughelaf, J. (2024). *A school's guide to implementation*. Education Endowment Foundation. Available at: https://educationendowmentfoundation.org.uk/education-evidence/guidance-reports/implementation.

Stewart, F. and Thompson, J. (2021). *Powerful knowledge as social justice*. CST. Available at: https://cstuk.org.uk/knowledge/thought-leadership/powerful-knowledge-as-social-justice/.

Vanhaecht, K., De Ridder, D., Seys, D., Brouwers, J., Claessens, F., Van Wilder, A., Panella, M., Batalden, P. and Lachman, P. (2021). 'The history of quality: from an eye for an eye, through love, and towards a multidimensional concept for patients, kin, and professionals', *European Urology Focus*, 7(5), 937–939.

CHAPTER THREE
ADVANCING EDUCATION: FIVE PRINCIPLES FOR INCLUSION

By Ben Newmark and Tom Rees

Foreword by Leora Cruddas

Whereas the previous chapter focused specifically on trust-led school improvement, and proposed a conceptual model, this chapter looks at how we can build school cultures in which all our children feel that they belong. We need to think hard about how we create school environments where all children flourish, ensuring both the optimal continuing development of their intellectual potential and their ability to live well as rounded human beings. This means a relentless focus on high-quality, inclusive education – advancing education for *all* our children.

At the highest level, I believe inclusion means that every child has the right to quality education and learning, and that all children feel like they belong in our schools. Alternatively, we cannot claim that our schools provide high-quality education if this is not true for all our children.

While it is helpful to adopt the broadest definition of inclusion, we need to be specific about which groups of children our school system is working less well for. This includes:

- children with special educational needs and disabilities (SEND)
- children who are living in poverty and those living in destitution (food poverty and shelter insecurity)
- children in the care system and those with a social worker
- children who are deemed to be young offenders and those at risk of offending, including children involved in gangs
- children experiencing mental ill health
- children living with acute health needs
- unaccompanied children seeking asylum and those fleeing violence
- children living in families where there is domestic violence or drugs, in unsafe homes and those experiencing trauma.

The list attempts to capture the range of experiences of our children for whom the system may not be working, but there will be others not captured within this list. The point is that all children have a right to high-quality education and to feel like they belong in their schools and communities.

This is particularly urgent for children with special educational needs and disabilities (SEND) and those from economically disadvantaged backgrounds, where the gap between them and their peers has opened up again.

One of the papers I am most proud of publishing (with Ambition Institute) is 'A good life: towards greater dignity for people with learning disability' (Newmark and Rees, 2022). Ben Newmark and Tom Rees argue that we need a broader and more ambitious vision of what a good life is. Human flourishing and dignity for all requires us to place greater value on things such as contribution, difference and the process of learning and work itself, to balance the meritocratic values of academic credentials, occupational status and wealth. The standard of education we expect for those who find learning hardest should be characterised by the same high expectations and intellectual rigour that society demands for our most able children. As in the previous chapter, this is something that requires action – to move our schools forward in a purposeful way.

Of course, we need structural and funding reform of our system of special educational needs and disabilities. We need further investment so that we can eradicate gaps between those children impacted by economic disadvantage and poverty and their peers. We need fundamental changes to the assessment system so that dignity is at the heart of all assessment. We should continue to make this case purposefully and intentionally to government.

But we can also focus on the schools and trusts we lead. We can commit to building strong educational institutions that address some of the inequalities and hardships we face as a society and as a nation. And we can commit to these institutions working together in a single moral purpose – to advance education for all the children in our schools – to create equal social and educational value for all children.

This chapter is an abridged version of the paper 'Five principles for inclusion' (Newmark and Rees, 2023). Like the paper, it is authored by Ben Newmark and Tom Rees. I think the five principles resonate not just in relation to special educational needs and disability, but much more widely as a blueprint for inclusive schooling.

Introduction

A child with a disability has the right to live a full and decent life with dignity and, as far as possible, independence and to play an active part in the community.

United Nations Convention on the Rights of the Child (Article 23)

Education in England does not work well enough for children identified with SEND. The challenge isn't new. Since the beginning of mass schooling, our education system has struggled with the challenge of including all children in a positive and meaningful way.

Some efforts of past societies are shocking to us today. At its most extreme, up to the 1950s some children with intellectual disability were not sent to school at all and were instead placed in asylums or institutions. The post-war movement ended such obvious segregation. Since then, through changes to the law and movements of integration and inclusion, the right of all children to a high-quality education until at least the age of 16 has been established.

Despite this obvious progress, however, our national system is in crisis. There is no alternative way of describing an education system not working for too many children and their families. There are underlying structural challenges that have a huge impact on the daily experience and life prospects of children with SEND, which must be acknowledged and addressed.

None of this is easy. If the solution for creating a more inclusive education system were obvious, we would have found it by now. We recognise that school and trust leaders often feel they are navigating competing priorities: whether that's balancing the needs of a majority group compared to a few individuals, or achieving good headline performance measures while maintaining inclusive practice.

A note on language

Special educational needs and disabilities (SEND) is an umbrella term used to identify and describe children who require extra help and support to be successful in school. Under the umbrella sit those with physical disabilities, those with identified learning disabilities and others without a formally identified condition.

The term is problematic; it suggests a binary between children with and without SEND. It implies these children are fundamentally different from the norm, and that their struggles are a product of these differences rather than the systems and structures around them. This can lead to beliefs and practices that exclude these children from aspects of education taken for granted by other children.

This does not mean all children will learn at the same speed if the systems and structures around them are changed to better meet their needs. Some children – particularly those with learning disabilities – will always find learning harder than most other people. While this disability is not their identity, it is part of it, and a properly functioning education system must support learning while affirming them as complete, unbroken humans. A depressing result of this framing is how many families have come to feel that the only way in which they can access support is to themselves categorise their children as deficient through processes – like education, health and care plan applications – that require them to demonstrate failure to get the help they need. This goes against the instincts of parents and families, and can be humiliating and degrading.

Second, the term SEND implies a commonality of experience. This is misleading and obscures the individual identities of those assigned the label. This leads to generic policy and strategy, and can expose children to inappropriate practice.

We know that while language matters, juggling terms is not enough. Language changes rapidly, but lived experience remains the same. We are also keenly aware that a focus on language and terminology can distract from what really matters – better outcomes for children who need these now.

After much debate, and recognising its limitations, we decided to stick with the term SEND. This designation is still used to direct resources towards children who need extra support, and without it, thousands of young people would find themselves without the help they need. We still live in the hope, nonetheless, of a long overdue retirement of this term, as more specific and expert practice leaves it without purpose or function.

In the meantime, we will continue to strive to find more precise language, and to focus more on how to meet children's learning needs than on their diagnosis.

Principles for inclusion
1. Dignity, not deficit Difference and disability are normal aspects of humanity – the education of children with SEND should be characterised by dignity and high expectation, not deficit and medicalisation.
2. Greater complexity merits greater expertise All children deserve a high-quality education – where extra support is needed, it should be expert in nature.
3. Different, but not apart Encountering difference builds an inclusive society – children with different learning needs should be able to grow up together.
4. Success in all its forms Success takes many forms – we should value and celebrate a wide range of achievements, including different ways of participating in society.
5. Action at all levels Change happens from the bottom up as well as top down – everyone has the agency and a responsibility to act.

Principle 1: Dignity, not deficit

Difference and disability are normal aspects of humanity – the education of children with SEND should be characterised by dignity and high expectation, not deficit and medicalisation.

Every child is an individual existing within the broad range of humanity. While some children need more help than others, everyone is complete in themselves and of inherent equal value.

Society distinguishes between what is considered normal and what is considered different, and those labelled with SEND are often framed as deficient or lacking – deviations from a constructed norm.

Children with SEND can still be subject to segregation within mainstream school settings and frequently receive teaching from less qualified teachers (Webster, 2022), and expectations of what they can achieve are often too low.

Clearly, this is unacceptable. Our schools should show there is value in difference, and no shame in finding learning harder.

Achieving this goal is made challenging by the medical model of disability, which positions people as disabled due to their 'impairments' or differences, focusing on what is 'wrong' or different. The system is set up this way: from education, health and care plans to disability living allowances, vulnerable children and their families are often required to provide evidence of failure to access support.

As SEND specialist Barney Angliss points out: 'it often seems the only way for young people with SEND – or their parents and carers to get help ... is to characterise themselves as "impaired", somehow less' (in Wespieser, 2021).

The medical model is not inherently wrong – it can help those who have a specific disability that they can and wish to change, such as epilepsy that can be fixed through surgical intervention if this is what a person wants. But there are many situations when the medical model is not appropriate.

Increasingly, our school system labels children with low attainment as having 'SEND'.

Currently, around four in ten children within the school system will be classified this way at some point in their school journey (Hutchinson, 2021). Clearly this is too big a proportion to respond to through specialist or personalised intervention; we need to be able to meet this broad range of need within regular mainstream classes.

The combined impact of over-medicalisation and capacity pressures means we need to take a different approach. Our education system should challenge framing that locates problems within children, rather than within approaches to teaching them.

Under the social model of disability, the way society is organised is positioned as the disabling factor – it focuses on what someone needs, and on provision aimed at removing barriers that prevent their inclusion and participation.

These philosophies manifest in our attitudes to difference. For example, asking, 'How do we support this child to read fluently?' instead of stating, 'They can't read fluently because of their diagnosis.'

One of the challenges for schools is that labels can become a self-fulfilling prophesy, with low expectations resulting in poor outcomes (Jussim and Harber, 2005).

Whereas labels and categorisation can lead us to reach too quickly for provision that is 'additional and different', this principle emphasises the need to demand higher expectations of teaching for those who need it the most. This requires us to strengthen the main teaching offer and to ensure that high-quality teaching is itself the intervention.

When a child's needs are being met with inclusive design, the label becomes less integral to their educational experience.

An increasingly inclusive and expert school and classroom environment helps children with SEND to learn better – but it also helps everyone to learn better.

As Nicole Dempsey says: 'The high quality, expectations, accountability and drive we offer for most of our students is the right of all students, but the individualisation, responsiveness and care that is often reserved for our SEND students is the right of all students too' (Dempsey, 2022).

The Alltogether Learning Disability Project[5]

Too few children encounter the stories of those with learning disability in their school curriculum.

Children with learning disability rarely see themselves in what they learn. This can easily create a sense that education is not really for them.

While there has been a welcome focus on diversity and differences around gender, nationality, religion, race and class in recent years, the voices of those with learning disability are often not heard.

Ben Newmark – a history teacher, school leader and the father of a child with learning disability – and Shaun Webster MBE – an accessibility expert with a learning disability himself – decided to do something about this.

Ben and Shaun worked together to create a school history curriculum telling the story of the inclusion and exclusion of people with learning disabilities from the prehistoric period to the present day.

The project grew to encompass two versions of the booklet, a teacher guide, and an audio podcast with the script adapted and read by people with learning disabilities.

The content – written with the help of historians, teachers and those with personal experience – shows how learning ability and disability are societal constructs not empirical binaries; that everyone's degree of ability and disability is contingent on how far they are included; and the process of inclusion involves everyone in society.

---

5   http://www.learningdisabilityhistory.org/.

Principle 2: Greater complexity merits greater expertise

All children deserve a high-quality education – where extra support is needed, it should be expert in nature.

Teaching children with special educational needs should be a sought-after responsibility that teachers see as high prestige. Children with SEND typically make less progress than their peers, yet they are often taught by less qualified staff. This is back to front.

In many professions, the hardest tasks are reserved for those with the greatest expertise. The association of prestige with complexity can be seen in the status of consultant surgeons, master craftspeople or special forces.

Expert practice for those with SEND is both an intellectual pursuit and a moral and professional responsibility, rather than an act of generosity or a demonstration of kindness. High expectations and expert teaching and support are the entitlement of all children.

Sadly, all too often, children with SEND are placed at the bottom of the educational hierarchy, with their education marked by lower standards, lower expectations, less scrutiny, and the perception that those who work with these children are engaged more in roles of care and charity than they are in knowledge-based expert professional practice.

This is damaging and untrue. Work with children who find learning difficult requires at least as high a level of ambition and expertise than work with the most academically able.

Better inclusion would lead to schools providing expert support for all children – characterised by expert decisions based on the best available evidence.

Professionals in the most inclusive schools and systems are recognised and rewarded as truly expert practitioners. They are given the time and resource they need to meet the needs of the children they are responsible for and to. Their leaders see their work as central to institutional professional goals and are as deeply invested in the educational and social progress of children with SEND as they are in the progress of children without.

Expert practitioners and leaders do not accept practice just because it is the way things have been done before. They are proactive and brave, willing to have difficult conversations when these are in the interests of the children they are responsible for.

Principle 3: Different, but not apart

Encountering difference builds an inclusive society – children with different learning needs should be able to grow up together.

Inclusion is important to get right for children with SEND. It is also important for the wider benefit it can bring to society. Being an inclusive society requires normalising difference, and proximity is an important piece of the puzzle.

If we rarely meet people who are different to us, they can seem unusual. Encountering difference can engender more accepting and positive attitudes. Where someone has a relationship with a person with a disability – whether a family member or colleague – they are less likely to hold negative attitudes towards disability in general. They are also more likely to have a perception of prejudice that matches the experiences of people with disabilities (Dixon, Smith and Touchet, 2018).

Schools can create proximity by prioritising integration both within mainstream schools and between specialist and mainstream provision. Currently, too few children in mainstream schools have meaningful interactions with those in special schools, and SEND departments within mainstream settings can often feel disconnected. The effect of this can be to locate the problem of inclusion in the excluded and imply they must change to be welcome in mainstream society – as if they have to reach a certain level in order to be welcome and included.

Achieving the right balance is hard. Specialist provision is necessary for some children. This can (but does not necessarily) reduce the chance of relationships being formed between children with SEND and those without. Building regular interaction between mainstream and specialist settings can be challenging, and requires determination and commitment from school leaders.

It's not a given, however, that including children with SEND in mainstream school will guarantee meaningful interactions between children with different learning needs. Approaches such as setting, in-class grouping or withdrawal interventions – while often introduced for good reason – can create segregation reinforced by a misleading binary between those considered 'normal' and those considered 'special'.

It doesn't have to be this way: many special schools, specialist provisions and mainstream schools build meaningful, ongoing partnerships. And mainstream schools can take some simple steps to reduce the perception of difference by employing interventions that help all learners, including those with SEND.

Great schools plan inclusion by design.

Teachers who are inclusive by design plan a lesson with those who struggle the most in mind. In every part of the lesson the pupils with additional needs are at the forefront of their decision-making. For example, the teacher breaks knowledge down into small chunks and plans how they will check for learning after each new piece of content. This strategy helps the pupils in their class with additional needs, but also all pupils benefit from the approach.

Inclusive schools see inclusion as core business: it is built into the fabric of the school, not bolted on at the end. They know that centring the school around those that find learning hardest benefits all children.

Working together, we can get to a place where we no longer hear teachers or headteachers say, 'I'm not an expert in SEND.' SEND provision should not be a secret garden: good teaching for those with SEND is in most cases good teaching for all (Davies and Henderson, 2021).

Pupils with SEND, whether in mainstream or specialist settings, should not be treated as fundamentally different to others. Through their actions, schools can reduce segregation and create plentiful opportunities for interaction.

Frank Wise Special School

At Frank Wise Special School every child up until the age of 16 has half a day a week working in partnership with their peers in a local mainstream school – a feature of its practice for more than 40 years. At post-16 the curriculum is constructed in a way that places off-site education at the heart of what they do, to ensure that students can apply their knowledge and skills beyond school, interacting and engaging with the other members of the local community.

Well aware of the systemic barriers to inclusion their pupils face, the school's leaders have spent years working to build opportunities for pupils in mainstream education and wider society. Joint headteachers Simon Knight and Heidi Dennison are aware of the dangers of locating inclusion challenges within their pupils, and have helped the organisations they work with better understand what their pupils can bring to mainstream schools, the workplace and the wider community.

Staff at Frank Wise school work closely with those in local mainstream partner schools to identify shared goals focused on the needs of the children involved. This can mean considering how different facilities or additional equipment could be used to enhance the curriculum, or how a shared activity could benefit the academic or social development of those taking part. The purpose of any project is considered carefully before beginning, and its success monitored and evaluated.

Wherever possible, visits between schools are reciprocal, with those from mainstream settings shown how they gain from accessing the curriculum, resources and spaces at Frank Wise. This demonstrates the benefits of inclusivity for everyone and helps fight benefactor–beneficiary modes of thought.

Inclusion is supported by building close links with the private sector, working with employers to ensure students get access to work experience and developing organisational understanding of how to effectively support people with their learning needs.

School staff are always looking to find new ways to enable members of wider society to understand what Frank Wise's students can offer, and to reduce the extent to which this information can be doubted. This has resulted in the production of digital business cards accessible by QR codes, annotated photo books evidencing the application of knowledge and skills, and CVs highlighting what the young person can do, alongside the support required to enable them to maximise their potential beyond school (Knight, 2022).

The work of the team at Frank Wise shows how meaningful inclusion and greater proximity can make society stronger and fairer.

Principle 4: Success in all its forms

Success takes many forms – we should value and celebrate a wide range of achievements, including different ways of participating in society.

Education needs a broad and ambitious vision of what a good life is. Schools play an important role in opening doors for children so that they have choice and opportunity in their life; exams and qualifications play an important role in this.

At the same time, we need schools to be places that value the intrinsic worth of each individual child, who is more than just their GCSE grades, and celebrate success in all its forms.

As expressions of society, schools are vulnerable to amplifying a narrow set of values based on wealth, professional status and academic credentials. It is common for schools to celebrate extraordinary academic achievement through assemblies, award evenings and prize-giving ceremonies.

High-profile alumni are often invited back to schools to inspire and motivate, often with tales of elite sporting and musical success.

Of course, there is nothing wrong with marking such achievements; a focus on academic outcomes is certainly not misplaced. But if these aims become too dominant, schools can become exclusionary to children for whom such accomplishments are not appropriate or realistic. This does not mean lowering standards but recognising that success can look different.

If we mark only conventional achievements, we imply those who don't rise to the top of prestigious fields have not succeeded. This is unimaginative and untrue. While credentialist and status-based achievements can contribute to good lives, good lives are not dependent on them.

Inclusion means building communities that affirm and value a wide range of achievements and experiences. It means noticing the extraordinary successes in the completion of everyday activities for those who have worked hard at them, and celebrating different ways of participation in society without condescension. It means understanding these things need not be in tension with each other – that acing spelling tests and learning to eat independently for the first time can both be impressive achievements, and that entry to Oxbridge and achieving an apprenticeship at a local firm are both dignified steps into adulthood to be celebrated – when we learn to properly value people as complete individuals who start at different points.

To do this meaningfully, schools need to pay close attention to the voices of all those who attend them, and to hear and value the ambitions of young people and their families.

In doing so, schools can broaden their conception of good lives and open them up to more people.

They can enrich communities by showing the importance of noticing and celebrating the achievements of all members, and not just a constructed elite. They motivate everyone to participate.

Principle 5: Action at all levels

Change happens from the bottom up as well as top down – everyone has the agency and a responsibility to act.

Everyone working with children, including school leaders and individual teachers, has the power to advance inclusion and improve the educational experience and outcomes of children with SEND. School systems are expressions

of wider societal values, and achieving inclusion within them is difficult. It is easy to feel downhearted, as parents become increasingly frustrated, and even the government's own review admits a long list of seemingly intractable problems with the SEND system.

Policymakers must prioritise making these changes, and those who understand the challenges should absolutely be advocating for that systemic change. But children get only one shot at school, and they can't afford to wait for system reform, which takes years to enact and with no guarantee of success.

A constructive debate about a better future requires us to focus on what we *can* change more than on what we *can't*. For more than 10 years, schools have been trying to achieve the goal of being a 'self-improving system'. Within this context, we should accept responsibility for thinking hard and taking action.

Schools contain high levels of expertise, and with sufficient resolve and direction have the ability to better include more children. Yet many teachers don't feel confident supporting learners with SEND (Ginnis et al., 2018); in fact, this is the area where trusts say they will encounter the most challenge (Jackson et al., 2022).

It is clear that school and trust leaders can do more to enable the profession to feel confident to meet this challenge. This has to start with training and development: school leaders can make sure that the training they are providing is based on the best available evidence on what works for children with SEND (Davies and Henderson, 2021).

Headteachers could familiarise themselves with the evidence base on best practice in SEND, starting with the EEF's guidance documents.

There is scope for everyone working at every level in the education system to learn more, and to improve provision and outcomes. We should be ambitious in our vision for a better future, and pragmatic about the journey to get there.

The momentum we need will begin with recognising the agency we have and the responsibility to use it. If we wait for others to move before we move, we will forever remain stuck where we are.

River Learning Trust

River Learning Trust, an academy trust of 28 schools, places meaningful inclusion at the heart of everything it does. One of its three guiding principles is 'everyone learning' – this means offering a rich and excellent educational experience regardless of academic ability, social background or special educational need. There is a commitment to the development of fully inclusive cultures within the trust's schools and this is emphasised with headteachers, other leaders and in communication to all colleagues.

At River Learning Trust, the role of SENDCO is positioned as strategic and central to developing classroom practice, and its place in the ladder to headship is deliberately emphasised. Trust leadership has made it clear this is an expert teaching role and not just coordination, promoting with headteachers that SENDCOs should be enabled to spend at least 50% of their allocated time in classrooms, working alongside teachers to support children and young people who find it hardest to learn. To make this possible in challenging financial times, the central team is working collaboratively with local authorities to develop innovative ways to minimise the bureaucracy of the role and support the wider system to better meet the needs of children and young people with SEND.

To recruit potential SENDCOs, and best prepare colleagues for this role, the trust delivers annually an 'Aspiring SENDCO' course. This programme repositions the priorities of the role to have an emphasis on teaching and learning, identifying to prospective SENDCOs the responsibilities of all staff and the importance of ensuring distributed leadership of SEND.

At River Learning Trust, enacting a distributed leadership of SEND is not the sole responsibility of the SENDCO. Katherine Walsh, director of inclusion, provides guidance and training to all trust staff – teachers and teaching assistants at individual schools, subject leaders, pastoral leaders, SENDCOs, headteachers, governors and the central team. This enables SENDCOs to work alongside other senior leaders to identify and implement a distributed leadership of SEND in their setting, independent of school size or individual context.

Across River Learning Trust schools, the needs of children with SEND are viewed as collective and shared, with the responsibility for developing and sharing specific strategies with teachers a core function of the SENDCO role. Within the distributed leadership of SEND, a teacher's role is exemplified as part of the graduated approach. Alongside the child and their family, the teacher's observations are essential in assessing potential barriers to learning and determining appropriate provision for a child or young person with identified, or potential, SEND needs.

The importance of language is emphasised in all trust communication. The use of phrases such as 's/he is SEND' is directly challenged, as these labels do not promote a holistic understanding of a child. Teachers and leaders are encouraged to break down the challenges children can face in the school or home environment to a granular level – for example, teachers are encouraged to focus on the difficulty children have in sustaining attention, rather than only on the identification or label, and are supported to better understand how to overcome this challenge. This approach is truly inclusive, as it places institutional focus on what is helpful for all children, not a separate group who need to be treated as if they were fundamentally different to their peers.

River Learning Trust chief executive Paul James is conscious of the constraints that can make inclusion feel hard, but strives to create momentum by building a culture that encourages teachers and leaders to focus on what they can change, and not what they can't. Keenly aware that children get only one go in the school system, he says: 'We can't wait for the national change to come; we are the adults in the room.'

Our responsibility

We have a responsibility – all of us – to make inclusion real; to offer more children more chances to feel successful and to realise dreams and aspirations that are as vital and important as anyone else's.

Nowhere is perfect, and the contested nature of inclusion means there will always be some difference of opinion on what good inclusion is. This chapter will be differently interpreted and understood, and identifying strong, replicable practice will involve robust discussions in good faith. Through these discussions we hope to learn more.

References

Davies, K. and Henderson, P. (2021). *Special educational needs in mainstream schools*. Guidance report. Education Endowment Foundation. Available at: https://educationendowmentfoundation.org.uk/education-evidence/ guidance-reports/send.

Dempsey, N. (2022). *What is the SEND system for?* Ambition Institute. Available at: https://www.ambition.org.uk/blog/what-is-the-send-system-for/.

Dixon, S., Smith, C. and Touchet, A. (2018). *The disability perception gap*. Policy report. Scope. Available at: https://www.scope.org.uk/campaigns/disability-perception-gap/.

Ginnis, S., Pestell, G., Mason, E. and Knibbs, S. (Ipsos MORI) (2018). *Newly qualified teachers: annual survey 2017*. Department for Education. Available at: https://assets.publishing.service.gov.uk/media/5b8e6cc6ed915d1eda528768/ NQT_2017_survey.pdf.

Hutchinson, J. (2021). *Identifying pupils with special educational needs and disabilities*. Education Policy Institute. Available at: https://epi.org.uk/ publications-and-research/identifying-send/.

Jackson, I., Jenavs, E., Evans, C., Rollett, S. and Muijs, D. (2022). *National CST school trust report*. Edurio. Available at: https://cstuk.org.uk/knowledge/ guidance-and-policy/national-cst-school-trust-report-2022/.

Jussim, L. and Harber, K. (2005). 'Teacher expectations and self-fulfilling prophecies: knowns and unknowns, resolved and unresolved controversies', *Personality and Social Psychology Review*, 9(2), 131–155.

Knight, S. (2022). *In pursuit of a life well lived*. CST. Available at: https://cstuk. org.uk/news-publications/cst-blogs/in-pursuit-of-a-life-well-lived/.

Newmark, B. and Rees, T. (2022). *A good life: towards greater dignity for people with learning disability*. CST and Ambition Institute. Available at: https://cstuk.org.uk/knowledge/guidance-and-policy/a-good-life-towards-greater-dignity-for-people-with-learning-disability/.

Newmark, B. and Rees, T. (2023). *Five principles for inclusion*. CST and Ambition Institute. Available at: https://cstuk.org.uk/knowledge/discussion-and-policy-papers/five-principles-for-inclusion/.

Webster, R. (2022). *The Inclusion Illusion: How Children With Special Educational Needs Experience Mainstream Schools*. UCL Press.

Wespieser, K. (2021). *The ResearchED Guide to Special Educational Needs: an Evidence-informed Guide for Teachers.* John Catt.

CHAPTER FOUR
STRATEGIC GOVERNANCE

One of the primary reasons I believe in the potential of school trusts is the capacity for strong strategic governance. The need for governance exists any time a group of people come together to accomplish an end. And what can be more important than the education of children and young people? The governance literature proposes several definitions, but most rest on three dimensions: authority, decision-making and accountability. I have adopted the working definition of the Canadian Institute on Governance, which has the following dimensions (Institute on Governance, 2024):

- Who has power?
- Who makes decisions?
- How do other players make their voices heard?
- How is account rendered?

The education system in England is complex, with high levels of school autonomy but also, somewhat paradoxically, high levels of centralisation at system level, with government involved far too much in operational detail. However, in a system where the majority of schools are run by autonomous legal entities, governance is essential. Those responsible for governance must ensure that, corporately, the trust board is *effective*, *accountable* and *ethical*. These three principles underpin the CST's work on governance.

As I said in chapter one, ultimately the task of governance in school trusts is to advance education for public benefit. This is a task bigger than one person – bigger than the executive trust leader – because we are all fallible – we all have moments of blindness alongside our capacity for insight. It is a task so important that it requires a group of people. The trust board.

Executive leaders hold their authority, power, legitimacy and ability to make decisions because these are delegated by the trust board. And their first line of accountability is to the trust board.

The proposition of trust governance

The proposition of governing a school trust is fundamentally different from governing a maintained school. For a start, those responsible for governance are directors under company law and trustees under charity law. They are

therefore bound by these legal frameworks, which are not the same for maintained school governors. The board is the 'responsible body' for the schools in the group. In most (but not all) cases, it is the local authority not the governing body that is the responsible body for schools they maintain. The trust is also the employer – again in most (but not all) cases, it is the local authority that is the employer for maintained schools. Trusts operate under a range of legal and regulatory frameworks that are not the same for maintained schools – for example, they are required to have annual financial audits and to publish accounts with Companies House. The task of governance is complex in that the board is responsible for a group of schools and the structures of governance are composite, requiring a scheme of delegation.

I could go on describing the differences, but I simply want to make the factual case that trust governance is fundamentally different from maintained school governance. We lose sight of this at our peril. This is why, in 2021, I thought it necessary to codify the proposition of governance, locating it in the legal, technical and regulatory frameworks that govern school trusts (CST, 2024).[6] To muddle the propositions of governance, or suggest that trust governance and maintained school governance have the same strategic functions is not only inaccurate but dangerous. Without domain-specific knowledge of school trust governance, trustees will be hampered in carrying out their role.

The Academy Trust Governance Code

In the latter part of the pandemic, it seemed to me that if we were to mature as a sector, we needed to define the standards of governance for ourselves. CST is a charity and the CST board had adopted the Charity Governance Code, a sector-led, voluntary code for charities. Importantly, the Charity Governance Code is neither legal nor regulatory. It sets the principles and recommended practice for good charity governance.

I thought that the emerging sector of school trusts (which are exempt charities principally regulated by the Secretary of State for Education) might benefit from such a code. Trusts operate in a particular legislative and regulatory environment and have some features that make them distinct from other types of charities, so I started working with the Chartered Governance Institute to think about developing our own governance code. Together, we set up a sector-led process for developing such a code.

We worked together with a steering group of sector-based organisations over a period of two years, with both the Department for Education and the

---

6   This guidance is updated annually.

Charity Commission acting as observers to the process. We launched a public consultation on the Academy Trust Governance Code in the summer of 2023 and published the final code in the autumn of 2023.

The Code supports existing good practice and encourages further reflection and progress. It is not only aspirational for school trusts, but also an acknowledgement of the power and significance of governance. Good governance leads to better outcomes for trusts, for our regulators and funders, and crucially, for our staff and pupils.

The Academy Trust Governance Code (ATGC, 2023) sets the principles, indicates desired outcomes and gives guidance on implementation for effective governance. It does not, however, look to repeat detailed regulatory requirements as set out in statutory guidance. It is intended to be a tool for continuous improvement in trust governance. It recognises that governance practice can operate in different ways depending on a range of factors, including each trust's structure, geographical spread, number of schools and sponsor status.

The Fundamental principle

The code begins with a fundamental principle: that those responsible for governance within school trusts are aware of and accept the Seven Principles of Public Life, understand the legal, regulatory and contractual obligations they must meet, and adhere to the statutory guidance published by the Secretary of State for Education. So the fundamental principles directly reinforce *effective*, *accountable* and *ethical governance*.

Those responsible for governance in a school trust are both trustees in charity law and directors in company law. Some boards refer to those who govern as trustees, and others directors, so in this chapter I refer to trustees/directors to ensure that all those responsible for governance recognise their roles and responsibilities.

The code's starting point is that all those responsible for trust governance:

- are committed to the trust's charitable object/s and are determined to deliver the trust's purpose and aims
- understand their roles and legal responsibilities, and have read and understood the Articles of Association, statutory and regulatory guidance and, in the context of voluntary academies, guidance from the relevant foundation
- are committed to effective governance and contributing to the trust's continued improvement.

Separate to the code, in CST's own guidance on 'Governing a school trust' (CST, 2024), we have published an ethical matrix to ensure good decision-making, based on the Seven Principles of Public Life (GOV.UK, 1995), as reproduced in the table below.

Selflessness	All our decisions have been taken in the public interest.
Integrity	We have not acted or taken decisions in order to gain financial or other material benefits for ourselves, our family or our friends.
Objectivity	Our decisions have been taken impartially, fairly and on merit, using the best evidence and without discrimination or bias.
Accountability	We are comfortable submitting ourselves to external scrutiny.
Openness	We have taken decisions in an open and transparent manner.
Honesty	We have been truthful in our actions, decisions and reporting.
Leadership	We have demonstrated the highest standards of public life in our individual and corporate behaviour.

The Financial Reporting Council has published risk factors for poor decision-making (Financial Reporting Council, 2024). These include:

- a dominant personality or group of directors on the board, inhibiting contribution from others
- insufficient diversity of perspective on the board, which can contribute to 'groupthink'
- excess focus on risk mitigation or insufficient attention to risk
- a compliance mindset and failure to treat risk as part of the decision-making process
- insufficient knowledge and ability to test underlying assumptions
- failure to listen to and act upon concerns that are raised
- failure to recognise the consequences of running the organisation on the basis of self-interest and other poor ethical standards
- a lack of openness by the executive, a reluctance to involve directors or a tendency to bring matters to the board for sign-off rather than debate
- complacent or intransigent attitudes
- inability to challenge effectively
- inadequate information or analysis
- poor-quality papers
- lack of time for debate, and truncated debate
- undue focus on short-term time horizons
- insufficient notice.

Good decisions do not happen by accident, and are the cornerstone of good governance. Good decisions depend on good judgement, a consideration of the available evidence and, where necessary, seeking expert and/or external advice. Good decisions also take a longer-term strategic horizon and consider macro-trends affecting school trusts.

The seven principles of the Academy Trust Governance Code

I would encourage you to look carefully at the whole code (ATGC, 2023). I cannot do it justice here, but I can provide a summary of the seven principles of the Academy Trust Governance Code:

Principle 1: Delivering the academy trust charitable objects Charities, including academy trusts, exist to fulfil their charitable objects. Charity trustees/directors have a responsibility to understand the environment in which the trust is operating and to ensure it fulfils its charitable object/s as effectively as possible with the resources available.
Principle 2: Leadership Strong and effective trust governance ensures the trust adopts a strategy that effectively and efficiently achieves its aims and charitable object/s. It also sets the culture for the trust, including its vision, values and desired culture.
Principle 3: Integrity Delivering the trust's charitable object/s should be at the heart of everything the board does. This may involve the board making decisions that are difficult or unpopular. Trustees/directors should show the highest levels of personal integrity and conduct, in accordance with the Principles of Public Life. To achieve this, the board and executive leadership team should create a culture that supports the trust's values, and adopt behaviours and policies in line with these values, setting aside any personal interests or loyalties.
Principle 4: Decision-making, risk and control The board is accountable for the decisions and actions of the trust. The board can delegate authority and powers but not accountability. Where the board has delegated functions, it needs to implement suitable financial and related controls, performance oversight and reporting arrangements, to make sure it oversees these matters effectively. The board must also identify and assess risks and opportunities for the trust and decide how best to deal with them, including assessing whether they are manageable or worth taking.
Principle 5: Board effectiveness The board provides a key role in ensuring that the trust thrives. The tone the board sets through its leadership, behaviour, culture and overall performance is critical to the trust's success. It is important to have a rigorous approach to the board's recruitment, conduct, performance and development.

Principle 6: Equality, diversity and inclusion
Advancing equality, diversity and inclusion helps a board to make better decisions. This requires commitment and should help a trust to understand the communities and pupils its schools serve and to deliver its charitable object/s. Equality and diversity are only effective and sustainable when the board works to be inclusive, guaranteeing accessibility to ensure that all trustees/directors are welcomed, valued and able to contribute to the charitable object/s and adhere to the agreed values of the trust.

Principle 7: Openness and accountability
The public's confidence that a trust is delivering high-quality and safe educational experiences in meeting its charitable object/s is fundamental to its success, reputation , and by extension, the success of the trust sector. Making accountability real, through genuine and open two-way communication that celebrates success and demonstrates willingness to learn from mistakes, helps to build trust and confidence, and earns and maintains legitimacy.

The code is a significant step towards the maturing of the trust sector, showing that we can set the standards of governance for ourselves.

Equality, diversity and inclusion

I want to draw out the sixth principle of our code because I think it is so important. The board should support governance at all levels to have a focus on equality, diversity and inclusion. This means ensuring the schools in the trust meet the three aims of the Public Sector Equality Duty: to eliminate unlawful discrimination, harassment and victimisation; advance equality of opportunity between people who share a protected characteristic and those who do not; and foster good relations between those who share a protected characteristic and those who do not. Specifically, there must be a focus on advancing equality for pupils, which for me is both a moral imperative and a social justice issue.

However, in this section I want to focus specifically on governance itself – to shine a light on the composition of our boards and the governance community. A study conducted by the National Foundation for Educational Research (NFER) on behalf of the Department for Education in 2020 found that a minority (just 3.5%) of respondents to its governance survey identified as Black, Asian and Minority Ethnic (Kettlewell et al., 2020). According to the 2021 census, the total population of England and Wales was 59.6 million, and 81.7% of the population was white (GOV.UK, 2022, updated 2024), so it is accurate to say that there is a problem with the diversity of our boards.

This is important not only as an equity or social justice issue but also, as Matthew Syed has so powerfully demonstrated, because a lack of diversity creates a form of collective blindness:

The critical point is that solutions to complex problems typically rely on multiple layers of insight and therefore require multiple points of view. The great America academic Philip Tetlock puts it this way: 'The more diverse the perspective, the wider the range of potentially viable solutions a collection of problem solvers can find'.

Syed (2019)

At the beginning of this chapter, I wrote that the need for governance exists any time a group of people come together to accomplish an end. And what can be more important than the education of children and young people? I would like to amend that here to reflect that governance is way more powerful and effective if we can marshal a *diverse* group of people. As Syed argues, diversity in fact leads to excellence. A key priority for us as we develop the governance of our trusts is to diversify.

Diversifying governance

Joy Sajuwa is a chair of governors at a large secondary school within the Unity Schools Partnership Trust, serving a large, ethnically diverse community. Joy was the second diverse governor on the board. She was also the first and (at the time of writing in August 2024) the only African-Caribbean chair within the trust.

She is also deputy headteacher in Havering of a three-form entry local authority primary school – and one of only two diverse members of staff in a school with 70% ethnically diverse students. On a wider scale, she is the only diverse member of staff with African-Caribbean heritage to hold a senior leadership role in the school and in the borough.

Of course, this is not the case for all staff groups within trusts and indeed for trust boards or governing boards. Some staff groups are more diverse and some boards are more diverse, but many or most are not. Joy offers some helpful approaches to address the challenge of board diversity.

She writes:

> A question was posed to us on the day of our trust chairs' meeting: 'Why is it that there is such a small representation of our diverse

---

community among the chairs of this trust?' The room was a little silent, but a truth had been unearthed. Everyone scanned the room for three seconds, which seemed like a very long three minutes. Then discussions began ... about the demographics of the schools served by the trust; about the need for more creative recruitment and outreach; about the need to reach those who at times would feel that their 'faces do not fit'.

First, why this is important. Having leaders who represent the community that we serve is itself a form of inspiration and aspiration for our pupils. For staff and parents to effectively communicate, understand and respond to specific concerns and issues, it helps to remove cultural barriers.

Shared experiences and cultural trust are essential tools to create an environment of effective communication and relationship building.

There are specific strategies every trust can take to reach out to under-represented communities. It requires, first and foremost, dispelling any assumptions and misconceptions surrounding the role of being a trustee, governor and even chair.

Here are some effective and quick win strategies for improving diversity in recruitment within governance and education as a whole. This is not exhaustive, but it is a start.

1. **Advertise in local newspapers aimed at diverse ethnic groups:** To ensure your outreach efforts are targeted and culturally relevant, advertise in local newspapers aimed at people from Black, Asian and minority ethnic groups. You will reach members of these communities who would otherwise never hear about opportunities to become governors.

2. **Engage with community centres, churches and mosques:** Actively participating in community events held at these centres can provide an opportunity to engage with individuals who may be interested in becoming governors. By building relationships and networking within these communities, you can foster trust and increase the likelihood of recruiting diverse candidates.

3. **Utilise the parent community:** Engage with parents' associations, parent–teacher associations (PTAs), or other groups within schools, to reach out to parents who may be interested in becoming governors. These individuals have a strong vested interest in education and can bring diverse perspectives to the governing body.

4. **Collaborate with local organisations and associations:** Partnering with local organisations that focus on diversity, inclusion or minority affairs can greatly aid in recruitment efforts. These organisations can help spread the word, provide recommendations and support the selection process by referring potential candidates.

5. **Leverage social media platforms:** Utilise social media to promote the benefits and importance of diverse governance. Sharing success stories and testimonies from current diverse governors can help inspire others to pursue similar roles. Additionally, targeted advertisements and sponsored posts can help reach a wider audience within specific communities.

6. **Implement mentorship programmes:** Developing mentorship programmes can provide guidance and support to individuals from under-represented backgrounds who are interested in becoming governors. These programmes can help build confidence, provide resources and offer networking opportunities, increasing the chances of successful recruitment.

7. **Provide training and workshops:** Organise training sessions and workshops focused on governance roles, responsibilities, and skills. By offering these opportunities within minority communities, you can nurture potential candidates, equip them with the necessary knowledge and empower them to take on leadership roles.

By implementing these approaches, schools and trusts can begin the process of increasing the ethnic diversity of their boards and contributing to more inclusive and equitable schools and trusts. But that is just the start.

Local governance

I wrote at the beginning of this chapter that the proposition of trust governance is complex in that the board is responsible for a group of schools and the structures of governance are composite. So the chapter would not be complete without an exploration of local governance.

For the avoidance of any doubt, I believe that the local tier of governance is absolutely essential to effective governance of a complex organisation. While trusts have different approaches to the local tier of governance, it is essential that trusts are clear about which functions of governance are delegated. In some cases, the local tier of governance holds no formal governance functions and is advisory only.

The local tier of governance is essential for the following reasons:

- Local governors are the trust's ambassadors in the local community, and indeed hold deep knowledge of the community and its specific needs. This knowledge and understanding is essential to the trust board. It helps the board anchor the schools in their communities (more on community anchoring and the role of governance in chapter ten).
- Local governors can play a very important role in relation to safeguarding and safety, as they know their schools intimately and will, in many cases, have closer involvement in the school than the trust board.
- Local governors can play a very important role in understanding the experience of children in the school, with oversight of whether all children in the school feel like they belong and are learning and developing.

There is a range of names for local school committees. CST's guidance is that the naming of this tier of governance should reflect the functions that are delegated:

- **Local advisory committees or councils**: no delegated governance functions or powers – the advisory committee is tasked with meaningful engagement with parents and local communities.
- **Local school committees**: limited delegated governance functions (but no powers), for example scrutiny of standards, health and safety and safeguarding, and community engagement.
- **Local governing boards**: a fuller set of delegated functions and some powers, which may include some decisions over school-level finance.

There should be a continuous feedback loop between the trust board and local tier of governance so that the trust board has oversight of the effectiveness of the local tier of governance. There should be a strong sense of a single governance community with a shared sense of mission, vision, values and culture, a shared sense of purpose and the execution of the strategy set by the trust board.

Reimagining governance at Anthem Schools Trust
By Claire Pannell, director of governance – general counsel

What is trust governance? It used to be the case that we didn't really know the answer to this question at Anthem. Therefore, our governance was not strategic or purposeful, and other than some pockets of excellence, it is not clear what it was really achieving. We had no proper flow of information between local governance and trustees, and while many volunteers were working hard and with good intentions, there was inefficiency and significant duplication. The distance between our schools was seen as an obstacle we just could not get over.

This all started to change when Mohsen Ojja became our new CEO. Mohsen joined us with boundless energy and enthusiasm and a real passion for governance. He quickly appointed me as director of governance – general counsel and gave me a wide remit, and lots of support, to overhaul governance. Having governance represented on the executive team has been really important in facilitating strategic governance and enabling us to make the radical changes we needed to, at pace and in line with our trust mission, vision and values.

Genuine consultation and collaboration were key to obtaining stakeholder buy-in to reimagining our governance so that it complemented and supported our new education strategy and enabled us to be a strong trust. Through this consultation we collaboratively took advantage of the freedom provided to us as academies to design a new strategic governance strategy, which is:

- bold and brave, and in line with our values of integrity, collaboration and excellence
- based on what is right for now and our new education strategy, not what was done before
- clear – with defined responsibilities and no unnecessary overlap or duplication
- holistic – with information flowing effectively around Anthem to where it is needed, from classroom to boardroom and back again
- expert, professional and robust – providing quality assurance internally and externally.

Information flows not just from students to trustees, but the flow is holistic and continuous and flows back so that our stakeholders feel heard and valued – because they are, as can be seen through this diagram:

There are two key parts to the governance strategy:

1. Anthem Community Councils (ACCs)
2. Collaborative Review Days (CRDs).

Anthem Community Councils (ACCs)

The consultation process enabled us to define four key ACC remits:

1. Community, including the voice of students, staff, parents/carers and the community, as well as climate change.
2. Celebration.
3. Panel members, including permanent exclusion and suspension reviews, admission decisions, formal HR processes and Stage 4 complaint hearings.
4. SEND and inclusion, and safeguarding.

Each ACC now has the following ACC Champion roles, which work across the four remits above:

- Timi Champion – this is a student voice role, named after a student at St Marks School who helped develop the idea of having students sit on our ACCs directly; these positions are filled by two students per school (Year 2 being the youngest), responsible only for the first two remits above
- Staff Champion
- Parent/Carer Champion
- Community Champion
- Sustainability and Climate Change Champion
- SEND and Inclusion Champion
- Safeguarding Champion
- Faith Champion (for our faith school – based on feedback)
- German Champion (for our bilingual school – a new addition based on feedback).

We have removed some of the previous formalities, bureaucracy and duplication, to provide additional time for more targeted support and collaborative working. Minutes have been replaced by an ACC dashboard. The champions each complete a Summary Champion Report ahead of each ACC, with a summary of the efforts that have been made, actions to complete, and any lessons learned or ideas or successes to be shared. This provides focus for the limited time many of our volunteers have. Each champion also proposes a RAG rating for their area, which is moderated by the ACC team and recorded on the ACC dashboard.

Timi Champion reports are also summarised in a national Timi Champion Summary Report, shared across the governance community.

Collaborative Review Days (CRDs)

CRDs are integral to our governance strategy, working very much with schools to drive improvement in line with our education strategy. CRDs also offer a robust form of quality assurance for our education strategy. CRDs are one-day visits by a team of internal education experts, from across the Anthem national team and other Anthem schools, to review, support and challenge local-level school provision. The ACC chair and a trustee representative are invited to join – this has been invaluable in completing the loop and building trust and understanding.

The purpose of CRDs:

- Deep dive: we can obtain on-the-ground knowledge of what is working well in each school at local level and can be shared across Anthem, and what is not working so well and needs support and additional resource.
- Support and challenge: targeted support and challenge where it is most needed to drive up standards.
- Professional development for senior and middle leaders: staff can learn from other schools what is being done well and how improvements can be made, in addition to learning how to evaluate and help improve across settings.
- Quality assurance: Feeds back on the quality of education provision to the whole governance community and school community.

Schools are entitled to at least three CRDs per academic year, with the expectation that schools needing more support will receive six. More than 60 CRDs have now been carried out. Termly feedback is sought and has been overwhelmingly positive. The feedback has also enabled us to adapt and refine CRD processes on an ongoing basis.

The robust quality assurance provided by CRDs has enabled further creativity for local governance.

The last year has seen fast-paced implementation of the first year of this new governance strategy. We have gone through a period of rapid change management and have needed to remain focused, determined and positive to overcome obstacles and challenge. However, a year on from the initial consultation stage, we have successfully reimagined governance at Anthem and we have a fantastic team of champions whose hard work is now channelled strategically, helping us to maximise attainment and build cultural, social and emotional capital for every student.

The relationship between the board and the chief executive

In their book *CEO Excellence*, Dewar, Keller and Malhotra observe: 'Poorly managed, the relationship between the CEO and the board can devolve into a loss of trust and paralysing ineffectiveness' (Dewar, Keller and Malhotra, 2022). Maintaining the distinctiveness of the roles of board and executive team can help to create a healthy climate.

In chapter one, I used Patrick Lencioni's proposition of 'smart' versus 'healthy' organisations (Lencioni, 2012). I noted that Lencioni believes smart organisations are good at the classic fundamentals of strategy, marketing, finance and technology, which he calls the 'decision sciences'. He believes that is only one half of the equation, and that being a healthy organisation is often neglected. This means minimal politics, minimal confusion, high morale, high productivity and low turnover. Part of a healthy organisation and a healthy relationship between the board and chief executive that means minimal politics, minimal confusion and high morale, is to understand the distinctive roles of the board and executive leadership team. It is perhaps helpful to explore the roles in three different spheres: strategy, leadership and accountability.

Strategy

The board and the executive team, usually through an iterative process, set and champion a clear strategy for the trust, which aligns with the trust's charitable object/s and ambition, in a clear time horizon. The role of the chief executive is to lead the trust executive leadership team to create and implement an effective trust operating model, with clarity about the delivery of trust-level and school-level activities, that aligns with the strategy. Chapter one outlined different approaches to strategy – the point here is ensuring that the respective roles of board and executive are clear. Both the board and the executive team have a role in reviewing progress rigorously to ensure strategic alignment and effective implementation.

Leadership

The board appoints its chief executive, and should provide effective support and challenge to the chief executive and the executive leadership team. The board should have sufficient independence from the executive leadership to allow scrutiny of the organisation. The chief executive leads the executive team and ensures that the executive team acts within the levels of authority delegated by the board. The board and executive team should work in partnership to ensure effective relationships between them. The board and chief executive have an equal role in driving the right relationship. Relational trust and transparency are key to building a culture of trust and confidence.

Accountability

The chief executive is accountable first and foremost to the board. The board also holds the executive leadership team to account for the effective implementation of the trust strategy and operating plan, including in relation to the use of resources and the drivers of impact. The board must assure itself of the integrity of financial information and that there are robust risk controls and risk management systems. Finally, the board must assure itself that there is compliance with regulatory, contractual and statutory requirements. The chief executive and executive team set the annual operating plan and budget, and implement effective operational systems to deliver on the trust's strategy. They deliver effective risk management across the key functions of the trust. They also ensure compliance with regulatory, contractual and statutory requirements.

Public interest, public servants and public institutions

I want to come full circle, back to the Canadian Institute on Governance, which I cited in the opening of this chapter. The Canadian Institute on Governance has a good governance triangle for the public sector (Canadian Institute on Governance, 2024):

- public interest
- public servants
- public institutions

The Institute on Governance believes that public-sector governance refers to the system of rules, processes and practices by which public institutions and organisations are managed and controlled. It states that the goal of good public-sector governance is to ensure transparency, accountability, efficiency and effectiveness in the delivery of public services.

It feels very important to restate my belief that trusts are public institutions, and that trust leaders are public servants who are the custodians and stewards of our state schools, serving a wider public interest. I explore this concept in greater depth in chapter six and return to it at the end of this book.

References

Academy Trust Governance Code (ATGC) (2023). *Welcome to the Academy Trust Governance Code website: a voluntary code for academy trusts in England*. Available at: https://atgc.org.uk/.

Canadian Institute on Governance (2024). *Our governance approach: good governance triangle*. Available at: https://iog.ca/about-us/our-governance-approach/.

CST (2024). *Governing a school trust*. Available at: https://cstuk.org.uk/knowledge/guidance-and-policy/governing-a-school-trust/. (Guidance updated annually.)

Dewar, C., Keller, S. and Malhotra, V. (2022). *CEO Excellence: The Six Mindsets That Distinguish the Best Leaders from the Rest*. John Murray Business.

Financial Reporting Council (2024). *Corporate Governance Code guidance*. Available at: https://www.frc.org.uk/library/standards-codes-policy/corporate-governance/corporate-governance-code-guidance/.

GOV.UK (1995). *The Seven Principles of Public Life*. Available at: https://www.gov.uk/government/publications/the-7-principles-of-public-life/the-7-principles-of-public-life--2.

GOV.UK (2022, updated 2024). *UK population by ethnicity: population of England and Wales*. Available at: https://www.ethnicity-facts-figures.service.gov.uk/uk-population-by-ethnicity/national-and-regional-populations/population-of-england-and-wales/latest/.

Institute on Governance (2024). *About us*. Available at: https://iog.ca/about-us/.

Kettlewell, K., Lucas, M., McCrone, T., Liht, J. and Sims, D. (2020). *School and trust governance investigative report*. NFER. Available at: https://assets.publishing.service.gov.uk/government/uploads/system/uploads/attachment_data/file/924898/NFER_Governance_Strand1_Report_FINAL.pdf.

Lencioni, P. (2012). *The Advantage: Why Organizational Health Trumps Everything Else In Business*. Jossey-Bass.

Syed, M. (2019). *Rebel Ideas: The Power of Diverse Thinking*. John Murray.

CHAPTER FIVE
OPERATIONS AND WORKFORCE

In the previous chapter, I explored the role of strategic governance and the importance of the chief executive in creating and implementing an effective trust operating model, with clarity about the delivery of trust-level and school-level activities, that aligns with the strategy. In this chapter, I move on to a discussion of the importance of considering operational capacity and workforce excellence.

What is operational excellence?

In a 2023 podcast, McKinsey & Company proposed that next-generation operational excellence is more than doing things well. It's about uniting an organisation around a common purpose, process and systems (Iverson, Pujol and Wijpkema, 2023). In chapter one, I explored the core charitable 'object', or purpose, of most trusts in the country: to advance education for public benefit. Put simply, operational excellence is the enactment of this core purpose. It is creating the systems and processes that drive educational excellence.

The operational functions in a trust exist only to serve that purpose. They are not an end in themselves – they are the means to deliver the highest quality of education for all the children the trust serves. And they must never become dislocated from this core purpose.

If we accept that operational excellence is about the enactment of core purpose, then it is really a set of culture, behaviours and daily practices that are deeply tied to the trust's reason for existing.

McKinsey's operational excellence framework (Colotla, 2024) consists of five core elements:

1. **Purpose** that defines why the organisation exists, with a strategy to achieve it.
2. **Principles and behaviours** to achieve the strategic vision, and establish a culture of trust, respect and constant innovation.
3. **Management systems** in place that develop leaders, build competency and drive desired behaviours.
4. **Technical systems** that eliminate waste and deliver value.
5. **Technology** that augments human capabilities to continuously improve.

School trusts are still emergent, and concepts of operational excellence may, in many trusts, still be nascent or emerging. There is more work for us to do to define operational excellence in the trust sector.

Operating models

In 2023, when CST launched a professional community for chief executives, we built each session around one of the domains of a strong trust (Cruddas, 2023). The session on operational excellence was led by Lena Koolman, partner at McKinsey. She drew on McKinsey's work on strategy to explore 12 elements of an operating model, which goes far beyond traditional 'boxes' and 'lines' (Dobru et al., 2021). McKinsey's model asks trusts to consider a series of strategic questions to build their operational capacity:

Structure:

1. **Roles and responsibilities:** Who is responsible for what, and where are activities performed/decisions made?

2. **'Boxes' and 'lines':** How are people organised and what are the reporting relationships?

3. **Boundaries and location:** What are the key locations of the organisation and how are resources spread across these?

4. **Governance:** How are critical decisions made on how the organisation is run, including who decides?

Processes:

5. **Process design and decisions:** How are key processes structured and how are decisions made?

6. **Performance management:** How is performance measured and against what KPIs?

7. **Systems and technology:** What systems are put in place to support organisational activities?

8. **Linkages:** What processes/forums are put in place to enable information sharing, coordination and collaboration?

People:

9. **Informal networks:** How do we take advantage of social networks and communities to enable the organisation?

10. **Culture:** What behaviours and mindsets enable the strategy and drive performance?

> 11. **Talent and skills:** What talent is needed to make the organisation successful?
>
> 12. **Workforce planning:** What quantity and quality of different skills are needed?

McKinsey's research found that transformations that touched seven or more of the 12 elements of an operating model were three times more likely to experience a successful redesign. Of the 12 operating model elements, McKinsey says three stand out as having an outsized impact on organisational efficacy:

Governance: The structure, authority and membership of bodies that make critical decisions about the direction of the organisation and how it is run.

Culture: The organisation's health, particularly its ability to align, execute and renew itself faster than its competitors.

Workforce planning: The organisation's approach to ensuring it has the resources, capabilities and capacity required to deliver value.

McKinsey talks about the impact of operating model changes that drive 'connective tissue'. By this it means high-quality horizontal and group interactions.

The key to an effective operating model is therefore making a series of finely balanced decisions and judgements that reflect the maturity and scale of the trust. It would be wrong to suggest that there is single model of operational excellence. But the development of an operating model does need to be intentional, and does need to seek an optimal balance between consistency and self-determination.

In chapter one, I illustrated the importance of purpose and culture with a case study from Dixons Academies Trust. Dixons uses Lencioni's strategic questions to determine its purpose and culture. In answering Lencioni's fourth question, Dixons talks about aligned autonomy as the basis for its operating model:

It is fundamentally important to us that we share the same mission and values. All Dixons students and staff should benefit from our best collective practices. And we all benefit from the collective resources, brand and reputation of the Dixons Academies Trust. So why then do we retain the term autonomy? It is because we believe leadership and personal accountability are founded on ownership and self-direction. A culture of conformity kills innovation and drives away the best staff. And standardisation fails to respond to changing needs and fails to adapt to a changing environment. We think it is the concept of aligned autonomy that is the foundation of our success so far: we are aligned on our mission, vision and values – these are our non-negotiables. But because we are determined to create a healthy organisation, the people who work for us must also have agency and self-determination.

Dixons Academies Trust (2024)

Importantly, its model of aligned autonomy has changed over time, and will continue to change as the trust grows and develops. Operational models are not fixed in perpetuity. They must be agile and able to respond to growth, perturbation, and changing political, economic, social, environmental and technological changes.

It is also important that there is a robustness to every operating model. I use this term in its technical sense, as defined by Capano and Woo: 'Robustness is the capacity to maintain the functions of a system', particularly when uncertainties are encountered (Capano and Woo, 2017). We have lived experience of the need for robust operating models during the massive upheaval of the pandemic. We should be proud that, generally speaking, trust operating models stood this huge test, were able to flex to respond to need, and still maintain their functions. As Chris Day, Stanimira Taneva and Rose Smith demonstrated in their excellent research, 'System leadership in disruptive times' (2021), during the pandemic trust operating models came into their own in the support of children, families and communities.

The importance of people

Operating models are in service of an organisation's purpose, but also its people. Our people matter, hugely. I wrote in the Introduction to this book about the importance of education as human flourishing. I said that we need to think hard about how we create school environments where all children flourish. But we also need environments where the adults flourish. I cited Lynn Swaner and Andy Wolfe: 'Where there are few flourishing adults, there will be few flourishing children' (Swaner and Wolfe, 2021). So, we need to care deeply about our workforce.

Teaching is an ancient and perhaps the noblest of professions. Education is the building of who we can be as a society, and all those working in our schools shape the next generation – they shape minds, nurture potential and help children to lead good lives. The work of those who educate is fundamentally *meaningful.* And it is a privilege to do meaningful work – work that connects us with what it means to be human and to an ethic of professional service.

Teachers and schools are valued and trusted by parents and wider society. The Ipsos Veracity Index is the longest-running poll on trust in professions in Britain (Ipsos, 2023). Teachers feature in the top six most trusted professions.

And schools are essential public institutions at the heart of their communities. In some communities, the school is the last public institution left. The value of schools and schooling cannot be overestimated.

We have seen through the pandemic the value of schools to society. Although most schools in England were closed to many pupil groups (but remained open for the most vulnerable children and the children of key workers), teachers, leaders and support staff exercised a duty of care, responding to a wider set of needs in the community.

But this does not mean that current levels of workload are sustainable. And we must pay attention to the wellbeing of our teachers and all those working in education. This is a duty of care we must exercise as a principle in its own right – the ethics of being a good employer. But it is also important because of the recruitment and retention crisis we face. I write these words in the middle of a critical teacher recruitment crisis and at a point where the staff who support our most vulnerable children are finding better-paid, more flexible jobs elsewhere.

The National Foundation for Educational Research's (NFER) annual Teacher Labour Market Report monitors the progress the education system in England is making towards meeting the teacher supply challenge by measuring the key indicators of teacher supply and working conditions. In 2024, the sixth annual report (McLean, Worth and Smith, 2024) shows that teacher supply is in a critical state, representing a substantial risk to the quality of education. Initial teacher training recruitment is likely to continue to fall below what is needed to ensure sufficient staffing levels in schools. Meanwhile, the number of teachers considering leaving teaching increased 44% between 2021–22 and 2022–23. NFER states that ambitious, radical and cost-effective policy options are urgently needed to address these challenges.

Only governments can really pull the big policy levers in relation to teacher recruitment. But trusts, as employers, can make a major impact on the retention of our staff. As John Tomsett and Jonny Uttley argue in their book, *Putting Staff First*, 'the good news is that we can train, develop and improve teachers. The bad news we have too few and too many are leaving' (Tomsett and Uttley, 2020, p. 26). Tomsett and Uttley's book focuses both on professional development and leaders' role in minimising anxiety levels. And we have data that suggests our teachers and leaders are anxious and stressed. The Teacher Wellbeing Index gives us the worrying fact that 78% of all education staff are stressed (Education Support, 2023). Tomsett and Uttley's approach advocates creating 'schools that are humane places where bright, enthused colleagues want to work' (2020, p. 163).

The Education Endowment Foundation (EEF) recently reviewed the evidence base on school leadership, culture, climate and structure for staff retention (Nguyen *et al.*, 2023). There are three interrelated leadership approaches and associated practices highlighted in the report:

1. prioritising professional development
2. building relational trust
3. improving working conditions.

Longer-term investment in the school workforce is essential, but a stronger settlement is conditional upon a better argument. We should not look to government to solve all the problems we face – particularly in relation to workload and wellbeing. As employers, we have powerful agency to create better conditions and a better climate for our staff.

Prioritising professional development

EEF's rapid evidence assessment shows that prioritising professional development is key to retaining our staff. A growing body of literature also places educator professional development at the heart of efforts to improve the school system. The rapid evidence review finds that there are some practices that contribute positively to teacher retention in particular:

- providing constructive feedback to support teachers to innovate and work collaboratively to address specific challenges they may be facing
- giving teachers opportunities – and removing any barriers – to access professional development opportunities
- cultivating leadership potential by supporting early-career teachers to innovate in their practice or take part in mentoring opportunities.

Professional development is most effective in a school culture in which teachers feel supported, valued and trusted, and where leaders have thought carefully about how to protect the time needed to engage in professional development.

In 2022, I invited Jen Barker and Katy Patten from Ambition Institute to write a paper setting out the case for prioritising professional development in school trusts, the 'active ingredients' of professional development, and the role that trusts can play in the design and implementation of high-quality professional development through leveraging their *capacity* (scale and expertise) alongside their ability to control the *conditions* and *culture* in which teachers work and professional development takes place (Barker and Patten, 2022).

Barker and Patten observe that, in recent years, a 'consensus' had developed around what makes for effective professional development – for example, Hill and colleagues (Hill, Beisiegel and Jacob, 2013). Various researchers have argued for a combination of characteristics, which tends to include concepts like subject-specificity, collaboration, a sustained duration, active learning, external expertise and teacher buy-in.

Barker and Patten point to an important review paper published in 2020, in which Sims and Fletcher-Wood challenge this view, highlighting that there are instances of professional development programmes that have adopted all these characteristics but have not succeeded in improving teaching (Sims and Fletcher-Wood, 2020). They go on to explain why. First, the studies that researchers examined to derive these characteristics were small, dated and not sufficiently robust to allow strong conclusions. Second, within the research cited it is not always clear what specifically is causing the impact: knowing that, for example, many successful professional development programmes involve collaboration does not tell us that collaboration causes their success. We need to be able to connect evidence of impact with identifiable evidence of what specifically is causing it.

In a subsequent paper for EEF, Sims, Fletcher-Wood and colleagues go on to identify the characteristics of effective teacher professional development, through a systematic review and meta-analysis (Sims *et al.*, 2021). This groundbreaking paper led to the publication of the EEF's 'Effective professional development' guidance report (Collin and Smith, 2021), which offers four mechanisms:

- A: Building knowledge
- B: Motivating teachers
- C: Developing teaching techniques
- D: Embedding practice.

Steve Rollett writes that 'school trusts are structures with the potential to build and mobilise knowledge pertaining to school improvement' (Rollett, 2021). If school improvement relies upon improvements in the quality of teaching, then educator professional development is a serious priority for the system.

Trusts can and should leverage their potential for improving professional development with the aims of retaining staff, raising pupil outcomes and tackling educational inequality.

Building relational trust

In chapter one, I talked about the need for relational trust as part of building organisational culture. I cited Viviane Robinson, who defines leadership as using expert knowledge to solve complex problems while building relational trust. She believes strongly that people do not want to work for leaders or organisations they don't trust.

The authors of the EEF's report suggest that leaders should:

- demonstrate individualised consideration
- treat people with respect
- consider teacher [or staff] voice
- promote collegiality.

What is striking about this is that it is not rocket science. If we are to retain our staff, building relational trust in our organisations is core to the way in which we enact culture.

Improving working conditions

I do not think that workload should be viewed on its own, but rather as part of a wider set of conditions in our schools and trusts. We should not be focused on only the *transactional* nature of workload reduction. We should also be building *relational* cultures.

The EEF defines working conditions in schools as 'a variety of physical, organisational, sociological, political, cultural, psychological, and educational features of teachers' jobs'. Synthesising the findings of these relevant studies allowed the EEF to identify and categorise a range of leadership practices associated with the approach of improving working conditions. These include:

- supporting teacher professional agency[7]
- promoting collegiality in schools
- developing an equitable support and recognition system
- establishing an effective communication structure
- supporting teachers with student disciplinary matters.

---

7   The original evidence review uses the term autonomy rather than agency.

We should also not underestimate the influence of headteachers on their schools, as recent research from the Education Policy Institute (EPI) has shown (Zucollo *et al.*, 2023). While trusts set the culture of the group of schools, the headteacher controls to a large extent the climate within each school. The EPI report links an effective headteacher with outcomes for pupils, not just for staff. Therefore, valuing and developing our headteachers, and paying attention to their workload and wellbeing, is absolutely essential to our shared endeavour, and the success of our education system and the retention of our staff.

Ethnic diversity in the workforce

I want to turn now to a fundamentally important issue for us in the English education system – that of ethnic diversity in our workforce. Research by NFER, in partnership with Ambition Institute and Teach First, explores the representation and career progression opportunities in the teaching profession in England among people from different minority ethnic backgrounds (Worth, McLean and Sharp, 2022).

It finds evidence of under-representation of people from minority ethnic backgrounds that is most pronounced at senior leadership and headship levels, but largely driven by disparities in the early career stages, particularly initial teacher training (ITT).

- The most significant ethnic disparities in progression occur in ITT, where people from Asian, Black, mixed and other minority ethnic backgrounds are less likely to be accepted to an ITT course than their white counterparts. People from Asian, Black and other minority ethnic backgrounds are over-represented among applicants to postgraduate ITT, but these groups are under-represented among trainees entering teaching.

- Teachers from minority ethnic backgrounds are also less likely to stay in the profession or progress to leadership than their white counterparts.

- Disparities in progression between different ethnic groups vary between regions and training routes, and depend on the ethnic diversity of the senior leadership team (SLT). Ethnic disparities in ITT acceptance rates are significantly smaller in London than nationally but larger for promotion to senior leadership. Disparities are smaller in schools with diverse SLTs compared to schools with all-white SLTs.

This provides important insights for action to establish a more equitable profession in future. The report calls for two main actions:

1. Support leaders and decision-makers in ITT providers, schools and trusts to equip them to make equitable workforce decisions. In particular,

the NFER report encourages ITT providers to review their application and selection processes to pinpoint the extent, nature and causes of the lower acceptance rates experienced by applicants from minority ethnic backgrounds, and to act to address any inequalities at this crucial first stage of entry into the profession.

2. Monitor progress across the system towards equalising the opportunities for progression in teaching for people from all ethnic groups.

As I wrote earlier in this chapter about the wellbeing of our staff, creating cultures where all our staff feel that they belong and can make a difference is a principle in its own right – the ethics of being a good employer. However, it is important for so many other reasons. Perhaps primarily among these is that our children deserve to see people like them – the wonderful, rich diversity of human beings – in all our schools. As Funmilola Stewart writes in the case study in chapter two (p. 63), 'If we are truly committed to equality, diversity and inclusion, [our pupils] must be able to see it, understand it and feel it.'

Chiltern Learning Trust's approach to diversifying the workforce

Sufian Sadiq, director of teaching school experience at the Chiltern Learning Trust, reflects on the trust's journey towards diversifying the workforce

Six years ago, we acknowledged there was a problem. The data from multiple organisations suggest that there is a serious lack of ethnic diversity in our workforce. But the awareness of the problem within organisations is inconsistent and/or limited.

First, we paid attention to training and development, from the trust board through the executive and throughout the organisation. We started with training that focused on equity for all, and we tried to build a knowledge base and understanding of the importance of equity in the system. We also gave people the evidence that shows there is a problem with the ethnic diversity of our workforce. The training started with the premise that people want to do 'good' but that not everyone appreciates some of the hurt, bias and discrimination that their words or actions cause. This all takes time. Training is not a quick fix.

Second, we wanted to demonstrate the importance of culture and values. There is no magic bullet around diversity, equity and inclusion. Culture takes time to develop and takes time to embed across an organisation.

You can't buy culture or values in an 'off the shelf' package. And it can't be rushed. Values are lived, not laminated. We surveyed more than two and a half thousand people in our organisation and developed a set of values that matter to people.

Third, we focused on recruitment. One of the most uncomfortable things in our sector is the lack of ethnic diversity at the top table – possibly because this is the most visible. We decided we did not want to take the approach of positive discrimination, but we did want to be absolutely clear that change was necessary. We decided that we wanted to be attractive as an employer to diverse talent from minority communities – and indeed all talent in the communities we serve. In particular, we wanted to attract *teachers* from diverse communities. One of the ways we did this was to help our young people and alumni from our schools to see the value of teaching.

Our chief executive, Adrian Rogers, made it a priority early on that we needed someone at the top table that reflected our community. He recruited me. This meant that I could advocate in the community. I also advocate for this change in the wider sector.

In terms of recruitment, we have not spent a penny on big mainstream media outlets and job boards. We shifted our paradigm very early on. We decided we wanted to recruit people who lived close by – people in the community.

Fourth, we initiated a future leaders programme that allowed us to develop a pipeline of talent. We now have a tranche of assistant heads who reflect the communities we serve. In our most recent recruitment round, we recruited two headteachers and two deputy heads from a minority background. This is because they were the best candidates. The pursuit of equity is not at the cost of excellence.

Fifth, at Chiltern Learning Trust, the whole leadership team play an active role in the community. Our senior team all sit on local boards in the community. If you are on the leadership scale, you are expected to turn up to at least one event in the community. This is in our DNA, we turn up.

We think of it as not just opening our doors and stepping out, but opening our doors and letting people in. Schools can become silos that exist within the footprint of the town. Teachers can drive into the community to the school and teach within the school for years without knowing the community – without visiting a mosque or a food bank or a community centre.

Some years ago, one of our weakest schools, which was new to the trust, was in a difficult position. There were some very strong critics of the school in the community. We had a choice – we invited one of the strongest critics to be the chair of the local governing body. We harnessed the energy of negativity that existed within the community as a force for good – a force for change. We had to listen to tough conversations and highly critical people in the community. We wanted to be present – we wanted to hear what our harshest critics were saying. This is now one of the strongest schools within our trust.

These partnerships have been a huge investment, but the value our community has been even greater. We are deliberate about what we want our communities to say about us – our community know that we will listen, particularly if something is not right. And they also know that we will act on our feedback.

We have been very deliberate in the way we have sought over many years to ensure our workforce begins to better reflect the communities we serve – and to view our schools and our trust as a community anchor.

A people strategy

If our people are essential to educational and operational excellence, then one might conclude that every trust should have a people strategy. There is a trend in trusts at the moment to develop people strategies. Where these are effective, they are explicitly in service to the core purpose of the organisation – to advance education for public benefit. A people strategy is not an end in itself – and it should never be dislocated from the wider education strategy. A people strategy is *always* in service to advancing education.

There are of course different ways to approach the development of a people strategy. It could, for example, be built on the subheadings in this chapter: prioritising professional development, building relational trust, improving workforce conditions and diversifying the workforce.

Mandy Coalter sets out an approach to developing a people strategy using the four-pillar model in her book, *Talent Architects* (Coalter, 2018):

1. leadership, culture and climate
2. developing your people talent
3. pupil behaviour
4. manageable workload and wellbeing.

Ted Wragg's people strategy

Tamsin Frances, executive director of people, strategy and IT, tells the story of the development of Ted Wragg Multi-Academy Trust

In the summer of 2021, despite some good practice, our trust lacked a clear vision for its role as an employer, and had no people strategy or supporting workforce and succession plans. The key areas identified by staff as weaknesses in the trust survey included perceptions of 'the trust', leadership dynamics did not score highly, and feelings of overwork and lack of access to career opportunities were reported.

Our trust started work using Lencioni's critical questions. Having clarified why our trust exists, how it behaves, what it does and how it will succeed, we turned our attention to a people strategy. Our trust's people strategy begins with an ambition to be the 'Greatest place to work in the South West'; we articulate this by saying that we want our teams to love coming to work. To achieve this, our people strategy has three key elements:

1. Welcome great people
2. Retain great people
3. Develop great people.

Fundamentally, the first step on our trust's people strategy journey was to recognise the importance of heavily investing in the development of our leaders, with a key focus on culture. It was unashamedly clear that headteachers were the most vital role within the organisation, with their responsibility for setting the right culture for their schools, and therefore they should have the best possible development. This includes a clear definition of their role as a trust leader, half-termly external coaching and supervision, annual study tours and consultation, three-weekly headteacher professional development networks, expert support and advice from trust enablement services, and systems focused on reducing workload for headteachers. Succession planning was also introduced across all of our family of schools, and this informed the need for proactive development programmes such as Future Heads and Future SENDCOs.

Ofsted, the inspectorate, visited our trust in October 2022 to undertake a multi-academy trust summary evaluation. This is what it found:

> The trust's people strategy is impressive. Teachers and other staff have a well-designed programme of both training and development linked to their level of experience and aspiration. In particular, the aspiring headteacher programme enables the trust to identify people with headship potential and then offer them bespoke training to prepare them. Integral to this is ensuring that the aspiring headteachers fully understand, and live out, the trust's vision and values for when they move to headship. Staff at the trust are overwhelmingly positive about the support and development they receive.

Completion rates for the staff survey were 54% in 2021 and are at 78% in 2024. The overall results for the leadership dynamics topic in the survey are above the national average.

	Question	Result	National Benchmark 2023/24 overall	Difference	National Primary Benchmark 2023/24	Difference	National Secondary Benchmark 2023/24	Difference
Top 3 results against national benchmarks								
1	25) How reasonable is the amount of time you spend on marking and assessment?	65%	49%	+16%	47%	+18%	50%	+15%
2	24) How reasonable is the amount of time you spend on lesson planning?	63%	48%	+15%	40%	+23%	52%	+11%
3	28) How easy or difficult is it to get support with lesson preparation?	64%	51%	+13%	49%	+15%	51%	+13%
Top 3 results								
1	16) How comfortable are you asking colleagues for help when you need it?	93%	90%	+3%	91%	+2%	89%	+4%
2	15) How respected by your colleagues do you feel?	89%	85%	+4%	85%	+4%	85%	+4%
3	48) How clear are the Trust vision and values to you?	79%	77%	+2%	81%	-2%	76%	+3%

Our investment in leadership has paid off, with an increase in staff happy coming to work, and school cultures that show a reduction of workload for teachers and an improved perception of why they are stronger together.

This chapter began with an exploration of operational excellence. I used theory development by McKinsey & Company to consider operating models and how these need to reflect the maturing and scale of trusts. We then turned to the importance of our people, taking an in-depth look at the evidence from the EEF's rapid evidence review into the leadership practices that retain staff. Finally, we have explored the importance of a people strategy as part of educational and operational excellence.

The first five chapters in this book have explored trust leadership – leadership of your organisation. Having the domain-specific knowledge to lead an organisation is essential, but I believe not sufficient. This is because the challenges we face today are beyond the reach of single institutions. We need to look up and out beyond our organisations and to work with other civic actors for the wider common good.

References

Barker, J. and Patten, K. (2022). *Professional development in school trusts: capacity, conditions and culture.* CST. Available at: https://cstuk.org.uk/knowledge/guidance-and-policy/development-in-school-trusts-capacity-conditions-and-culture/.

Capano, G. and Woo, J.J. (2017). 'Resilience and robustness in policy design: a critical appraisal', *Policy Sciences*, 50(3), 399–426.

Coalter, M. (2018). *Talent Architects: How to Make Your School a Great Place to Work.* John Catt.

Collin, J. and Smith, E. (2021). *Effective professional development.* Guidance report. Education Endowment Foundation. Available at: https://educationendowmentfoundation.org.uk/education-evidence/guidance-reports/effective-professional-development.

Colotla, I., Fookes, W., Iverson, T., Schaefer, E., Sellschop, R. and Wijpkema, J. (2024). *Today's good to great: next-generation operational excellence.* McKinsey & Company, 19 January. Available at: https://www.mckinsey.com/capabilities/operations/our-insights/todays-good-to-great-next-generation-operational-excellence.

Cruddas, L. (2023). *Building strong trusts.* CST. Available at: https://cstuk.org.uk/knowledge/guidance-and-policy/building-strong-trusts/.

Day, C., Taneva, S. and Smith, R. (2021). *System leadership in disruptive times: robust policy making and enactment in school trusts.* CST. Available at: https://cstuk.org.uk/assets/pdfs/QR_system_leadership_in_disruptive_times_report_2021.pdf.

Dixons Academies Trust (2024). *Aligned autonomy.* Available at: https://www.dixonsat.com/why/aligned-autonomy.

Dobru, D., Hewes, C., Simon, P. and Welchman, T. (2021). *Operating model transformations: not all elements are created equal.* McKinsey & Company, 20 September. Available at: https://mckinsey.com/capabilities/operations/our-insights/next-generation-operational-excellence.

Education Support (2023). *Teacher Wellbeing Index.* Available at: https://educationsupport.org.uk/media/0h4jd5pt/twix_2023.pdf.

Hill, H., Beisiegel, M. and Jacob, R. (2013). 'Professional development research: consensus, crossroads, and challenges', *Educational Researcher*, 42(9), 476–487.

NEW DOMAINS OF EDUCATIONAL LEADERSHIP

Ipsos (2023). *Ipsos Veracity Index: trust in professions survey.* Available at: https://www.ipsos.com/sites/default/files/ct/news/documents/2023-12/ipsos-trust-in-professions-veracity-index-2023-charts.pdf.

Iverson, T., Pujol, F. and Wijpkema, J. (2023). *Operational excellence: how purpose and technology can power performance.* McKinsey & Company, 21 April. [Podcast] Available at: https://www.mckinsey.com/capabilities/operations/our-insights/operational-excellence-how-purpose-and-technology-can-power-performance/.

McLean, D., Worth, J. and Smith, A. (2024). *Teacher labour market in England annual report 2024.* Available at: https://www.nfer.ac.uk/publications/teacher-labour-market-in-england-annual-report-2024/.

Nguyen, D., Huat See, B., Brown, C. and Kokotsaki, D. (2023). *Reviewing the evidence base on school leadership, culture, climate and structure for teacher retention.* Education Endowment Foundation. Available at: https://educationendowmentfoundation.org.uk/education-evidence/evidence-reviews/leadership-approaches.

Rollett, S. (2021). *Communities of improvement: school trusts as fields of practice.* CST. Available at: https://cstuk.org.uk/assets/pdfs/ICE_10096_CST_School_Improvement_Whitepaper.pdf.

Sims, S. and Fletcher-Wood, H. (2020). 'Identifying the characteristics of effective teacher professional development: a critical review', *School Effectiveness and School Improvement*, 32(1), 47–63.

Sims, S., Fletcher-Wood, H., O'Mara-Eves, A., Cottingham, S., Stansfield, C., Van Herwegen, J. and Anders, J. (2021). *What are the characteristics of effective teacher professional development? A systematic review & meta-analysis.* Education Endowment Foundation. Available at: https://educationendowmentfoundation.org.uk/education-evidence/evidence-reviews/teacher-professional-development-characteristics.

Swaner, L. and Wolfe, A. (2021). *Flourishing Together: A Christian Vision for Students, Educators, and Schools.* William B. Eerdmans Publishing.

Tomsett, J. and Uttley, J. (2020). *Putting Staff First: A Blueprint for Revitalising Our Schools.* John Catt.

Worth, J., McLean, D. and Sharp, C. (2022). *Racial equality in the teacher workforce.* NFER. Available at: https://www.nfer.ac.uk/publications/racial-equality-in-the-teacher-workforce/.

Zucollo, J., Cardem Dias, J., Jimenez, E. and Braakmann, N. (2023). *The influence of headteachers on their schools*. Education Policy Institute. Available at: https://epi.org.uk/publications-and-research/the-influence-of-headteachers-on-their-schools/.

PART 2
CIVIC LEADERSHIP

Chapter 6:   The trust as a civic institution 123

Chapter 7:   Building a connected system..136

Chapter 8:   Catalysing collective leadership through a theory of action ..144

Chapter 9:   The protection and promotion of public values 154

Chapter 10: Community anchoring (by James Townsend,
             Ed Vainker and Leora Cruddas) 169

CHAPTER SIX
THE TRUST AS A CIVIC INSTITUTION

As I wrote in the Introduction to this book, if our children are to flourish, we need to work with other civic leaders for a wider common good. In talking to the Civic University Commission, I realised that school trusts are civic organisations too – just like universities and NHS trusts – so I started to talk and write about 'civic trusts' and civic leadership.

Public benefit

Throughout the first section of this book, I pointed to the charitable 'object' that most trusts have: the 'advancement of education for public benefit'.[8] I explored, in chapter two, the imperative to advance education. In this chapter, I want to look at the charitable object through a different lens – that of public benefit. Importantly, the core charitable object does not say to advance education *for the pupils your trust serves* – rather, it says to advance education for *public benefit*. One way of interpreting public benefit is that trust leaders have a duty to work with others to advance education as a wider common good.

For the avoidance of doubt, this does not mean that school trusts should try to become all things to all children and families. Trust leaders should never lose sight of the primary purpose to advance education. But it does mean that the trust leaders can and should work with other civic organisations and leaders to ensure that children and families can access coherent public services, that they are safe, that their welfare is protected, and they can contribute to wider civic, creative and cultural life.

Public benefit has a legal meaning and definition. In its guidance on public benefit, the Charity Commission (2013) offers the view that, in basic terms, public benefit is about knowing:

- what the charity is set up to achieve – this is known as the charity's 'purpose'
- how the charity's purpose is beneficial – this is the 'benefit aspect' of public benefit

---

8   For Catholic academies, the objects are specifically restricted to the advancement of the Catholic religion in the diocese. The public benefit requirement is set out in the 'conduct' of the academy. The 'public benefit requirement' fits within Catholic Social Teaching as a commitment to the common good.

- how the charity's purpose benefits the public or a sufficient section of the public – this is the 'public aspect' of public benefit
- how the trustees will carry out the charity's purpose for the public benefit – this is what is known as 'furthering' the charity's purpose for the public benefit.

There is a legal requirement on trustees to report on public benefit by providing a review in the trustees' annual report of the significant activities undertaken by the charity to carry out its charitable purposes for the public benefit. But this is not my primary interest here. The charitable purpose of trusts is potentially a powerful tool through which to tell the story of the trust's civic purpose:

- What does it mean in our trust to advance education?
- What public benefit/s do we want to deliver in relation to advancing education?
- What is the full range of ways in which our trust could carry out the charitable purpose (or purposes)?
- How could this form part of our wider narrative about the work of our trust?

One of the most advanced expressions of a civic trust working for wider public benefit is Ark, and the story of EdCity. Although beyond the reach of most school trusts, it is worth noting and celebrating this extraordinary achievement for the breadth and scale of its civic ambition.

Ark and the story of EdCity

Ark's charitable objects focus explicitly on closing the education gap, stating that it is 'an education charity that exists to make sure that all children, regardless of their background, have access to a great education and real choices in life'. It also states that Ark 'incubates, launches and scales ventures that share our mission and values'. It is this second part of its mission that has led Ark to found a nursery network and a curriculum programme and, most recently, to create EdCity.

Ark Schools is one of the larger trusts, with 39 primary, secondary and all-through schools. In the summer of 2020, the trust announced the go-ahead for plans to develop EdCity – an innovative, not-for-profit education and community hub in White City, West London. EdCity – a partnership between Ark and Hammersmith and Fulham Council –

will bring a range of social, educational and housing benefits to the local community.

The development will provide 132 homes for local people and key workers, including teachers. Unusually, these will all be social or affordable housing, with all the homes managed by the London Borough of Hammersmith and Fulham.

Alongside this housing will be a new Ark primary school building, a nursery, adult education facilities, the new Onside youth zone – WEST – and an office building that will be the home of the Ark network team and a hub for the education sector.

The hope is that this hub will bring a range of benefits from local to national. The community in this corner of White City will get the direct benefit of homes and new educational resources, and EdCity will contribute to the wider borough regeneration project focused around the White City Innovation District, which already benefits from the Imperial campus. But there is also a national scope. Ark's ambition is to create a new, affordable collaboration space for the education sector, which – especially post-Covid – has lost many of its spaces to meet and connect.

What is a civic institution?

The word 'civic' typically has two different types of definition: first, relating to a city or town – a place-based definition; second, relating to the duties or activities of people in relation to their town, city or local area – a leadership definition. I will explore both of these definitions.

In February 2019, the UPP Foundation Civic University Commission launched its final report, 'Truly civic: strengthening the connection between universities and their places' (UPP Foundation, 2019). The report sets out how universities have the capability, opportunity and responsibility to be civic partners and further support the places where they are based to solve some of their most pressing and major problems.

The late Lord Kerslake, then chair of the Civic University Commission, said: 'The deep economic and social changes that are happening in Britain today have, alongside Brexit, made the civic role of universities even more vital to the places they are located in' (UPP Foundation, 2019).

Since the publication of the Civic University Commission's original report in 2019, we have had a global pandemic followed by a period of significant geopolitical tensions and economic challenges. This has had an enormous detrimental impact on our children and communities.

As I highlighted in the Introduction to this book, the pandemic left us with multiple challenges, but we could not have anticipated those that would follow – a global economic crisis, climate disasters, social unrest, global political instability, and conflicts and wars – which are likely to determine our future.

So, it is ever more the case that the deep economic and social changes that are happening in Britain today have made the civic role of public institutions even more vital – not just to the places they are located in, but in leading a response to the renewal of our communities and of civic life.

We also know that the legitimacy of public institutions is crucial for building peaceful and inclusive societies. The United Nations says:

Trust is integral to the functioning of any society. Trust in each other, in our public institutions and in our leaders are all essential ingredients for social and economic progress, allowing people to cooperate with and express solidarity for one another. It allows public bodies to plan and execute policies and deliver services.

United Nations (2021)

A civic institution has the following features:

- It is deeply rooted in place.
- It understands in a deep way the things that are putting pressure on our children, families and communities.
- In addition to its core purpose (in the case of school trusts, this is to advance education), it understands that the challenges we face in society mean that it cannot be successful without working with other civic actors.
- It makes an explicit strategic commitment to working with other civic leaders for the wider common good.

Five principles

I first made the case for school trusts as a new form of civic structure in January 2020. I published a joint paper with Jonathan Simons, director at Public First, setting out an emergent civic trust framework. In this paper, we set out five principles that might be borne in mind for a school trust that is thinking about how it best delivers a civic role (Cruddas and Simons, 2020).

First, civic work has the most impact when it is delivered in partnership with other civic actors – local government, the NHS, housing bodies, cultural institutions, local businesses, and so on. There will be some areas where it makes sense for school trusts to take the lead, working with some or all of these partners. And there will be some areas where school trusts work to support initiatives or programmes that are led by others in a local area.

Second, work should be designed around what the local community or communities where trusts are based actually want and need. Any programme of work should be preceded by a period of active consultation with the community – with a particular focus on those more economically disadvantaged and marginalised groups who may find it harder to articulate their priorities and needs.

Third, work should be appropriate to the scale and the strengths of the trust and its partners. In general, larger trusts will be able to, and ought to think about, impact on a larger scale than smaller trusts. But all trusts are able to make a civic impact in some way.

Fourth, civic work should be a conscious part of a trust's activity. Real impact comes when it is seen as a core part of the trust's activity and strategy. This means that for civic work to be meaningful it should have an executive-level sponsor as well as support from the trust's board, and it should receive regular scrutiny from the trust to ensure it continues to be focused and useful.

Fifth, civic work should sit as part of the trust's broader strategy. It need not be a huge amount of additional work, nor should it require significant additional financial resource from the trust. There should be no conflict between the trust's broader charitable purposes to advance education and the civic work it engages in with its local community or communities.

The Windsor Academy Trust has civic impact explicitly as one of its 'Big Moves'. Its commitment exemplifies the five principles.

Windsor Academy Trust: driving education for the greater public good

At Windsor Academy Trust (WAT), our mission extends beyond the WAT Family. We believe in the power of education to create thriving communities, where all children – not just those in our schools – have the opportunity to succeed. Civic action is at the heart of our strategy and we take an intentional approach to enhance our role as a civic leader, driving positive change for the greater public good.

Our Civic Impact 'Big Move' focuses on three key areas: local communities, regional partners and national influencers. By collaborating with these partners and working through a six-step process, we aim to create lasting and meaningful impact in the communities we serve.

Through this Big Move, we are strengthening our commitment to social value, fostering educational innovation and, ultimately, empowering all children to reach their full potential.

We have established 'Civic Hubs' dedicated to the communities we serve. We are collaborating with other civic actors and anchor organisations, embracing civic leadership and co-creating the future of education.

Together, we can create a brighter future for all children and their communities.

Four tests

The Civic University Commission report identified a number of tests that it recommends universities apply to their work (UPP Foundation, 2019, p. 9). I have taken the four tests identified in the report and converted them into a series of tests for school trusts, as follows.

A public test:

- Do people talk about our schools with pride and awareness?
- Do children and parents feel a strong connection to our schools? Are our schools places where all our children feel they belong? How do we know?
- Do we know the things that are putting pressure on our communities?

A place test:

- Are our schools serving all of our children in this locality?

- How well do we know the places in which our schools are located? Do we have a working knowledge of the service provision, access, uptake?
- Do we understand/can we access data on the wider needs of the population – for example, what is public health data telling us about the population-level health issues?

A strategic test:

- Can we define where our civic boundaries are? What are the geographical areas we are primarily focused on?
- Is it clear how our trust is linked to local/regional leadership in the area? For example, do we know the boundaries of the local integrated care system and how these map to our civic boundaries?

An impact test:

- Do we have a clear analysis that informs our civic work? Can we clearly articulate what outcomes, impacts and benefits we want as a result of our civic work?
- Can we point to ways in which we have helped to develop capability (of people, organisations and communities)? Can we point to how we have connected multiple forms or resource to build capability?

The London & South East Education Group has pioneered an approach to social impact. It is a large, merged college group, university centre and 15-school multi-academy trust. The group delivers a wide range of education and skills provision across its region. London South East Academies Trust comprises primary, special and alternative provision schools, and London South East Colleges delivers further and higher education across seven campuses in London.

London & South East Education Group: measuring civic impact

By Louise Wolsey, group chief strategy officer

In 2019 we published our first group strategy. Unusually, we set out a bold and pioneering ambition as a collective to operate as a social enterprise. Our intent was to increase our social impact by thinking and operating differently. Civic leadership was central to this, and to our vision and ethos of how we deliver education. Through this approach we have now delivered £110 million of independently verified social value since 2019. This contributes to the social and economic mobility of children and families in the communities we serve, and greater social justice.

Towards civic impact

To us, 'place' matters. It is in our name and part of our identity, our reason for being. Based in and part of our communities, we play a key role in civic life. It's a responsibility we take seriously. We know place-based inequalities in England are deep-rooted and we want to play our role, leading locally as an education provider and major employer, in helping address these.

We know that education and skills play a much larger role than simply meeting national economic priorities and solving the productivity challenge. Education changes lives, opening up opportunities for children, young people and their families. It creates pathways to better-paid jobs and sustainable incomes that give families the stability they need to not just survive but to thrive.

Therefore, in forming our approach to civic impact, we considered how, as 'actors' in the civic space, we could contribute. The civic and social value models, while not new concepts, have made rapid progress in the public consciousness over recent years. We have seen since 2019 an increased emphasis on local 'place' in public debate across a range of public-sector organisations, including local and combined authorities, the NHS and universities. Within higher education, the Civic University Network movement continues to develop and is coming more to the fore with the financial pressures on the higher education system currently.

So, when we formalised our group structure and overarching strategy framework, we knew that we needed to find a new way of measuring impact beyond educational outputs, and a way of working that better utilised all the resources we have available.

Building on the Social Value Act in 2012, the work of Sir Michael Barber paved the way for further policy decisions in which the use of 'social value' was becoming an increasingly accepted way of articulating how public value could be created and, just as importantly, quantified and measured (Barber, 2017). To this end we chose to adopt a social value tool, the TOMs Framework, as an approach that we could embed in our strategy, policy, planning and implementation at every level of our work (Social Value Portal, 2024).

Delivering our civic responsibility as social value

We use the TOMs Framework, developed by the National Social Value Taskforce and Local Government Association, as a lens through which we codify our approach to civic leadership. We use it to classify and segment activity using these themes:

- promote growth of responsible and local businesses
- local skills and employment
- healthier, safer and more resilient communities
- decarbonising and safeguarding our world
- promote social innovation.

Using proxy financial values to quantify the positive social impacts approach provides a consistent way to measure and report social value, allowing comparisons over time and between organisations, and shapes our strategy going forward. In policy terms, the use of social value in central government procurement has increased further with the 2020 Social Value Model and it is increasingly being used as a tool in demonstrating a return on investment across government departments. As social justice becomes more central to policy, in addressing poverty and generational economic disadvantage, helping the public purse go further will be even more essential for the new administration.

Our impact

When we launched our 2019 Strategy Framework, our goals were defined with an overarching ambition, using TOMs to measure and articulate the impact of the group operating as a social enterprise. A year into the new strategy, we commissioned an external audit through the Centre for Local and Economic Strategies (CLES) to review progress alongside the Social Value Portal, which provided independent verification of our results. This ensured that the overall civic impact we articulate is robust and would withstand external scrutiny. Over the five years of the strategy, we have generated £110 million of social value.

A practical example of this approach and mindset includes our redevelopment of one of our sites in Greenwich. Working in partnership with the Mayor of London and the Royal Borough we have taken a deliberate approach to maximising social value in the local area. Working alongside housing association LandQ, our collaboration will create not only a new further and higher education campus but in addition 294 new homes, 51% of which will be affordable. The new campus, which will be completed in 2025, will provide new education opportunities for thousands of Londoners, and in addition will be a vital community asset with a new green community space and desperately needed homes for local people. This project was shortlisted as highly commended in the 2022 National Social Value Awards for Best Public Sector Project following the group being awarded the National Social Value Public Sector Leadership Award in 2021. Building on this, beyond the education sector the group was invited by the Greater London Authority and Bloomberg to shape the post-Covid London Recovery Board Anchor Institutions Impact Framework.

Next steps

Looking ahead, our new Group Strategy Framework 2024–2030 sets out how we are continuing this journey, meeting the challenges and opportunities facing us as an education group operating primarily in a globalised capital city in which extremes of wealth and inequity exist side by side. As a public institution and a large employer, with significant buying and influencing power, we have a key role to play in helping to address the challenge of social justice. In our view, creating and measuring social value provides a practical framework for achieving the ambition of social justice through supporting the design and development of projects and services that create tangible benefits for society. Our *why*, 'transforming lives through the power of learning', drives our focus not just on *what* we do (providing education) but *how* we do it.

In this regard, this approach has characterised the leadership role we have played over the past decade in leading SEND system improvements across our region, drawing on insight from both the CLEAR Framework for Leading Systems Change (Dreier, Nabarro and Nelson, 2019) and the work of Professor Frank Geels' 'Multi-level perspective on system innovation' (Geels, 2006).

The CLEAR Framework for Leading Systems Change describes five key elements of the systems change process:

1. Convene and Commit: Key stakeholders engage in moderated dialogue to address a complex issue of mutual concern. They define shared interests and goals, and commit to working together in new ways to create systemic change.

2. Look and Learn: Through system mapping, stakeholders jointly build a shared understanding of the components, actors,

dynamics and influences that create the system and its current outcomes, generating new insights and ideas.

3. Engage and Energise: Diverse stakeholders are engaged through continuous communication, to build trust, commitment, innovation and collaboration. Inspiration, incentives and milestones help drive progress and maintain momentum.

4. Act with Accountability: Shared goals and principles set the direction of the initiative, while measurement frameworks help track progress. Coordination and governance structures can be developed as initiatives mature.

5. Review and Revise: Stakeholders review progress regularly and adapt the initiative strategy accordingly. Adopting an agile, flexible, innovative and learning-centred approach allows for evolution and experimentation.

Joining the dots for SEND learners across the education system from school, through post-16 provision, and beyond to higher-level learning and employment, is creating a blueprint for progression pathways, using tried and tested strategies that improve job outcomes for vulnerable learners – a key to social equity and improved quality of life.

The learning and insight gathered through our journey has driven the development of our new foundation, demonstrating our enduring commitment to this agenda at scale – testing and growing consistent approaches to addressing educational, economic and social inequality in our communities and beyond. To this end, when it is right for us to lead, we do, and at other times we collaborate with partners who bring new strengths, 'doubling down' on our social enterprise ambition, which is now in our DNA, part of our mindset and 'how we do things'. It is helping us maintain the agility and innovation that have characterised our approach for the past five years, deepening this further as civic actors working in and on the system.

Definitions or expressions of the civic institution and civic leadership

I said at the start of this chapter that the word 'civic' typically has two different types of definition: first, relating to a city or town – a place-based definition; second, relating to the duties or activities of people in relation to their town, city or local area – a leadership definition.

The place-based definition is broadly how your organisation works with other civic organisations – the local NHS hospital and/or mental health trust, the university, the local authority, the police ... the list could go on. This work is about building a connected system locally and is explored in chapter seven. But it is also about catalysing collective action among civic leaders through a theory of action, explored in chapter eight. Place-based civic work is orientated towards action on behalf of children, young people and communities.

The leadership definition is rooted in a mindset of protecting and promoting public values. This is the theme of chapter nine.

In chapter ten, I come to a particular conceptualisation of the civic institution as an 'anchor institution' and an expression of civic leadership as community anchoring. In this definition, the partnership is not with other civic actors but with the community itself. It is about how we build relational trust with the communities we serve.

All of these different expressions or definitions of civic leadership are legitimate, but it is probably not possible for a trust or a trust leader to enact all of them all at once. So ultimately this is about prioritisation. The civic work of a trust can begin with modest action and build over time.

But mostly the civic mindset is driven by a belief that we can make a difference, that we are more powerful than we think we are.

References

Barber, M. (2017). *Delivering better outcomes for citizens: practical steps for unlocking public value.* Independent report led by Sir Michael Barber. HM Treasury. Available at: https://www.gov.uk/government/publications/delivering-better-outcomes-for-citizens-practical-steps-for-unlocking-public-value.

Charity Commission (2013). *Public benefit: an overview.* Available at: https://www.gov.uk/government/publications/public-benefit-an-overview/public-benefit-an-overview.

Cruddas, L. and Simons, J. (2020). *School trusts as new civic structures: a framework document.* Confederation of School Trusts and Public First. Available at: https://cstuk.org.uk/knowledge/discussion-and-policy-papers/school-trusts-as-new-civic-structures-a-framework-document/.

Dreier, L., Nabarro, D. and Nelson, J. (2019). *Systems leadership for sustainable development: strategies for achieving systemic change.* Harvard Kennedy School. Available at: https://www.hks.harvard.edu/sites/default/files/centers/mrcbg/files/Systems Leadership.pdf.

Geels, F. (2006). 'Multi-level perspective on system innovation: relevance for industrial transformation', in Xander, O. and Wieczorek, A.J. (eds), *Understanding Industrial Transformation: Views From Different Disciplines,* pp. 163–186. Springer.

Social Value Portal (2024). *Social value measurement.* Available at: https://www.socialvalueportal.com/measurement.

United Nations (2021). *Trust in public institutions: trends and implications for economic security.* UN Department of Economic and Social Affairs. Available at: https://social.desa.un.org/publications/trust-in-public-institutions-trends-and-implications-for-economic-security.

UPP Foundation (2019). *Truly civic: strengthening the connection between universities and their places. The final report of the UPP Foundation Civic University Commission.* Available at: https://www.upp-foundation.org/wp-content/uploads/2019/02/Civic-University-Commission-Final-Report.pdf.

CHAPTER SEVEN
BUILDING A CONNECTED SYSTEM

The previous chapter made the case that the trust is a civic institution. If that is true, then we must also accept that trust leaders are civic leaders. As well as leading a group of schools, trust leaders also look out beyond their organisations. They work with one another in a connected system, and they seek to work with other civic actors for the greater common good. This means that trust leaders ensure that they build local relationships, not just with each other but with wider civic actors – the local authority, the NHS trust, the mental health trust, health commissioners, the police commissioner, the university vice chancellor, etc. It is only through building a connected system that we will be able to address the multiple challenges facing our communities. This is place-based leadership.

The civic mindset and civic leadership

It is perhaps worth noting at the outset that a civic mindset is one that looks up and out, not just down into the organisation you lead. A civic mindset involves asking a few simple questions:

- What is putting pressure on the children, young people and communities my schools serve, and impacting negatively on their capacity to learn?
- The core purpose of schools is to advance education for public benefit, but what are the factors that may be mitigating against this?
- Who are the civic organisations or actors that need to work together to address this issue (or these issues)?

The civic mindset accepts that the complexity of social issues means that it is unlikely that a single public institution, acting alone, will be able to solve any particular issue.

The potential of leadership agency in connected systems – via a brief tour of complexity theory

The concept of connected systems is well established in the world of artificial intelligence. While we see and understand the benefits of connected systems in virtual worlds, we often fail to see those same benefits in real worlds.

The public sector is a series of isolated, complex adaptive systems. The complexity of each part of the public sector perhaps keeps us working hard within our own system. Complexity theory has been used to understand and analyse specific public-sector systems, but there is potential to think about how much more powerful these complex adaptive systems could be if we could find relational and integrative ways of working together.

Complexity theory typically focuses on the behaviours of individual 'agents' within systems and/or the collective behaviours of systems. I will not delve too far into the field of complexity theory here, but I am interested in how 'agents' in complex systems adapt in response to interactions with other 'agents', which for our purposes are leaders.

According to Holland, in complex adaptive systems, a small directed action can cause large predictable changes in aggregate behaviour through lever points (Holland, 2014). This is important, because I am not arguing here for the grand gesture. I am making the case for small directed actions.

Turning to the behaviours or qualities of complex systems, self-organisation and emergence are common to most descriptions. Rzevski and Skobelev state: 'Complex systems self-organise, i.e. autonomously change their behaviour or modify their structure, to eliminate or reduce the impact of disruptive events (adaptability) or to repel attacks (resilience)' (Rzevski and Skobelev, 2014, p. 9).

So if we accept that public-sector services can be described as complex adaptive systems, they can in fact self-organise. They can change their behaviours or modify their structures. They do this both to be more adaptable and more resilient. They do this through the agency of leaders. Davis and Sumara define self-organisation as spontaneously arising 'as the actions of autonomous agents [read leaders] come to be inter-linked and co-dependent' (Davis and Sumara, 2014, p. 5).

The second common behaviour or quality of a complex system in the literature is 'emergence'. The behaviour of complex systems emerges from the interaction of the agents (read leaders) in the system. Rzevski and Skobelev propose that emergent behaviour is unpredictable, at odds with Holland's view that a directed action can cause predictable changes in behaviour. However, both propose that emergent behaviour is not necessarily random in that it generally follows a discernible pattern – in essence, a new order.

It might follow, then, that the increased agency of leaders within systems may introduce higher complexity – and a new order (Rzevski and Skobelev, 2014, p. 7).

A critic may say that there is perhaps a need to undertake some form of evaluation of the validity of transferring concepts from the physical to the social sciences before analysing the usefulness of complexity theory to education. However, although complexity theory emerged from the physical sciences, it is fundamentally transdisciplinary. Part of the thought-liberation of complexity is the refusal to be constrained by the current order of things or the intellectual horizons imposed by the rigid classifications and, to quote William Blake, the 'mind-forg'd manacles' of a centrist world view.

Public-sector leaders are so much more powerful than we think we are. We do not have to wait for governments to tell us what to do. There is greater good – a higher purpose – of connected systems working for the children, young people and communities we serve.

The importance of relational trust

Viviane Robinson's work has helped us understand that the ability to build relational trust is a core leadership virtue. Relational trust is grounded in social respect – and respectful exchanges are marked by genuinely listening to what people say and by taking these views into account in subsequent actions.

One of the problems in enacting civic leadership is that we do not know each other. We do not understand what is putting pressure on us as leaders. We could probably broadly define one another's core purposes, but not with any nuance or real understanding. We do not know or understand the factors mitigating against the aims and purposes of our organisations, so we cannot explore in any real way whether working together may help us solve some of our problems.

One of the ways to overcome this problem is to build a relationship directly with another civic leader. In this approach, the leaders of the organisations build a relationship of trust, which then enables greater levels of inter-organisational trust. This is because an organisation cannot trust another organisation, but the leaders of organisations that trust each other can decide on resource prioritisation towards mutually defined goals. This can in turn lead to a situation where decisions and actions are made collectively, resulting from the orientation of trust among top management or leadership of each organisation.

There are some core benefits of building relational trust between civic leaders:

- It is the first step towards prioritising resources towards mutually defined goals.

- It can help public-sector leaders respond to issues of place and public concern, and potentially helps to deliver public benefit.
- It creates patterns of doing things that build organisational capability.
- It reduces the sense of risk associated with change.
- Leaders feel comfortable opening up their practice to others.
- Leaders are willing to talk honestly about what works and what doesn't.

Relational trust is the glue that helps us build a connected system.

A relational approach to building a connected system

The case study below charts the journey of trust between the chief executive of a school trust and the chief executive of an NHS trust. Initially, the relationship is focused on building trust through understanding some of the issues facing any chief executive. The relationship develops in a way that allows the two chief executives to explore mutual priorities and resource allocation towards those priorities.

Maximising public benefit and civic duty: collaborative partnerships between school and NHS trusts
Windsor Academy Trust

Collaboration between schools and NHS trusts transcends individual institutions, envisioning an ecosystem where education and healthcare no longer react to problems individually but co-create the future together. When executed effectively, it can profoundly impact communities and society. Both NHS and school trusts, as public-sector bodies, have a vital civic role to play as anchor institutions deeply embedded in their communities.

The NHS faces a significant challenge in shifting from a predominantly reactive healthcare system to one that proactively enhances overall wellbeing. With overwhelming demand and a shortage of healthcare workers, investing in long-term results becomes imperative. Simultaneously, in schools, good health and wellbeing among young people is critical in ensuring their academic and personal success. To overcome these challenges, collaboration is paramount.

Windsor Academy Trust's strategic collaboration with NHS trusts began when a meeting between our CEO and the CEO of a group of four NHS trusts took place following an introduction from a trustee who sat on both our school trust and an NHS trust board.

Conversations initially focused on seeking to understand more about each other's sectors and knowledge-sharing in areas such as strategy, financial sustainability and governance. Quickly, three strategic areas to focus collaborative endeavours were identified: preventing health issues in young people, establishing community health provisions on school sites, and developing the future NHS workforce.

Discussions underscored that a collaborative approach would yield the most meaningful impact over time. Education significantly influences health, and schools possess a unique capacity to shape societal behaviour and choices. To enact shared aspirations, it was crucial to establish a gateway connecting NHS trust CEOs with school trust CEOs, and headteachers and school-based civic leaders, to facilitate collaboration.

Our CEO and the CEO of the group of NHS trusts initiated efforts to connect local health and education providers in each of our geographic areas. This involved aligning and connecting other school and NHS trusts outside our own in order to facilitate this broader collaboration.

This approach has borne fruit, with Windsor Academy Trust forging meaningful partnerships with NHS trusts directly serving our school communities, including Midlands Partnership University NHS Foundation Trust, Sandwell and West Birmingham Hospitals NHS Trust, Birmingham and Solihull Integrated Care System, Stoke and North Staffordshire NHS Integrated Care Board and Walsall Healthcare NHS Trust.

Numerous initiatives, spanning prevention, community health services in schools and workforce development, are now underway.

As an example of this partnership in action, our free school, Windsor Olympus Academy, has partnered with Sandwell and West Birmingham Hospitals NHS Trust to establish asthma-friendly environments in school.

Students are now trained as 'asthma champions' to educate local primary schools about asthma triggers and treatment, and we have a longer-term aim of hosting an inoculation programme at the school. We have held a number of community workshops with the NHS in-school around topics such as healthy eating and the menopause. Now we are exploring partnerships with local doctors' surgeries to offer a centralised health agreement for the community.

Another project has seen NHS allied health professional careers fairs hosted at Windsor Olympus Academy to support our ambitions to diversify the workforce by bringing together healthcare professionals to inspire students and parents to consider a career in health. Furthermore, 50 of our students visited Birmingham Children's Hospital to spend a morning touring the wards, meeting staff and learning about the range of different job roles within the NHS.

We are also particularly proud to have been invited by the acting chief medical officer at Birmingham and Solihull Integrated Care System to be part of an initiative that is bringing health professionals and educators from across the city together, with the aim of reducing health inequalities in young people.

Meanwhile three of our secondary schools in North Staffordshire are working with the NHS's Mental Health Support Team to provide mental health education to students, wellbeing workshops for our staff and information evenings for parents, to create a whole-school approach to mental health.

In addition, we are working with the NHS's workforce development team in Stoke and North Staffordshire to develop a primary school careers pilot, which is being informed through pupil voice. This pilot looks at the many different roles within the NHS – clinical and non-clinical – with the content appropriately tailored for early years through to key stage 2. Once developed, this will then be trialled in our Stoke primaries before being rolled out to all primaries across the county.

Finally, in Walsall, we are working closely with Public Health to host a new NHS community healthy eating programme from our primary schools, providing a location for pop-up immunisation clinics, and supporting Public Health with an emotional health and wellbeing pilot aimed at primary school aged children.

Windsor Academy Trust's Community Foundation – a fund set up to support young people and their families in the community – will also play a role in these initiatives. Our annual fundraiser for the foundation, WAT a Run, which takes place during Mental Health Awareness Week, involves staff running two marathons in two days, while students take part in sponsored fun runs at their respective schools. The event not only raises vital funds for the foundation but helps deliver on our civic purpose by using physical activity to support both physical and mental health.

Neil Carr, CEO of Midlands Partnership University NHS Foundation Trust, aptly noted that school trusts are 'pushing on an open door' and, together, we can significantly impact communities. Aligning efforts will secure the wellbeing and prosperity of local communities while fulfilling trusts' civic duty.

In time, we hope the partnerships Windsor Academy Trust is developing will extend beyond education and healthcare as we work towards building interconnected, thriving communities where individuals' wellbeing and aspirations take centre stage. This collaborative approach serves as a beacon of hope and progress for the future of our society, echoing the words of Dr Martin Luther King: 'Whatever affects one directly, affects all indirectly.'

The civic mindset is a way of thinking about strategic relationships that are responding to issues of place and public concern. It is a way of thinking about how we use our professional agency to self-organise. In the above case study, we have focused specifically on the interrelationships between health and education. As we shall see in the next chapter, there are wider issues that would require different relationships and different forms of organisational connectedness.

This case study illustrates the point made by Senge and colleagues: 'Short-term reactive problem solving becomes more balanced with long-term value creation. And organisational self-interest becomes re-contextualized, as people discover that their and their organisation's success depends on creating well-being within the larger systems of which they are a part' (Senge, Hamilton and Kania, 2015).

In the next chapter, I will focus on how civic leaders create the conditions for collective impact by addressing complex problems affecting children and young people that require different actors to work together.

References

Davis, B. and Sumara, D. (2014). *Complexity and Education*. Routledge.

Holland, J.H. (2014). *Complexity: A Very Short Introduction*. Oxford University Press.

Rzevski, G. and Skobelev, P. (2014). *Managing Complexity*. WIT Press.

Senge, P., Hamilton, H. and Kania, J. (2015). 'The Dawn of System Leadership', *Stanford Social Innovation Review*, Winter. Available at: https://ssir.org/articles/entry/the_dawn_of_system_leadership#.

CHAPTER EIGHT
CATALYSING COLLECTIVE LEADERSHIP THROUGH A THEORY OF ACTION

With the passing of Nelson Mandela in late 2013, the world celebrated a remarkable life. But the spotlight on Mandela's accomplishments relegated to the shadows much of the reason that he has had such a lasting impact, in South Africa and beyond. Above all, Mandela embodied a system leader, someone able to bring forth collective leadership. ... At no time in history have we needed such system leaders more. We face a host of systemic challenges beyond the reach of existing institutions and their hierarchical authority structures.

Senge, Hamilton and Kania (2015)

The pandemic has left us with a host of negative legacies – educational, social, economic and related to health. On top of these challenges has come a global economic crisis that in England has resulted in more families living in absolute poverty. It is beyond the reach of individual organisations to support our families and communities through this. It requires a collective response.

Peter Senge has always influenced my thinking. Early in 2024, I re-read the beautiful piece on 'the dawn of system leadership' (Senge, Hamilton and Kania, 2015). Senge and his colleagues write about the importance of cultivating collective leadership in diverse settings around the world, even while our larger cultural contexts remain firmly anchored to the myth of the heroic individual leader. They write that 'undoubtedly we are at the beginning of the beginning in learning how to catalyse and guide systemic change at a scale commensurate with the scale of problems we face, and all of us see but dimly' (Senge, Hamilton and Kania, 2015).

Senge *et al.* propose that profound commitment to the health of the whole radiates to nurture similar commitment in others: 'Their ability to see reality through the eyes of people very different from themselves encourages others to be more open as well. They build relationships based on deep listening, and networks of trust and collaboration start to flourish' (Senge, Hamilton and Kania, 2015).

Capabilities to foster collective leadership

Concepts of collective leadership are not new – but they are enormously difficult to catalyse. Before I consider theories of action, I want to summarise three core capabilities for collective action outlined by Senge *et al.* (2015).

Senge, Hamilton and Kania's three core capabilities to foster collective leadership

The ability to see the larger system

In any complex setting, people typically focus their attention on the parts of the system most visible from their own vantage point. This usually results in arguments about who has the right perspective on the problem. Helping people see the larger system is essential to building a shared understanding of complex problems. This understanding enables collaborating organisations to jointly develop solutions not evident to any of them individually and to work together for the health of the whole system rather than just pursue symptomatic fixes to individual pieces.

Fostering reflection and generative conversations

Reflection means thinking about our thinking, holding up the mirror to see the taken-for-granted assumptions we carry into any conversation and appreciating how our mental models may limit us. Deep, shared reflection is a critical step in enabling groups of organizations and individuals to actually 'hear' a point of view different from their own, and to appreciate emotionally as well as cognitively each other's reality. This is an essential doorway for building trust where distrust had prevailed and for fostering collective creativity.

Shifting the collective focus from reactive problem-solving to co-creating the future

Change often starts with conditions that are undesirable, but artful leaders help people move beyond just reacting to these problems to building positive visions for the future. This typically happens gradually as leaders help people articulate their deeper aspirations and build confidence based on tangible accomplishments achieved together. This shift involves not just building inspiring visions but facing difficult truths about the present reality and learning how to use the tension between vision and reality to inspire truly new approaches.

Source: Senge, Hamilton and Kania (2015)

But simply catalysing collective leadership is unlikely to be sufficient. We will need to develop a collective theory of action. Viviane Robinson has perhaps done more than any other leadership academic to help to codify theories of action through agreeing on the problem to be solved, constructing a theory of action, evaluating the relative merit of the current and alternative theories of action, and implementing a new, sufficiently shared theory of action (Robinson, 2018). Albeit she views the theory of action through the lens of school improvement, her conceptual analysis and outline of process are very helpful in the context of civic leadership.

A problem orientation approach to catalysing collective leadership[9]

In the previous chapter, I wrote that it is worth noting that a civic mindset is one that looks up and out, and involves asking a few simple questions. Perhaps the most important of these is what is putting pressure on the children, young people and communities my schools serve?

This may generate a very long list of issues. Consider starting with one issue – it will perhaps be the issue that is uppermost in your mind – the intractable problem that is causing you the most worry, which could be particular to a school or across a group of schools. Then consider initially a small number of leaders of other organisations that may be necessary to solving this problem.

Finding the strategic focus

One of the problems we face as leaders, particularly in the current context, is the sheer number of issues affecting our children, young people and communities. So strategic thinking is needed in finding a focus and determining the scope.

Robinson observes that one of the dangers of ambitious leaders is that they tackle too many problems at once and overload themselves – so we need to discern those problems that are relatively more important. She also says that considerable work may be needed to gather the evidence and mount the arguments needed to settle on one or two strategic priorities (Robinson, 2023, p. 112).

Robinson also points to the importance of connecting the details with the big picture. She cites Henry Mintzberg:

It is [leaders'] ability to bounce back and forth between the concrete and the conceptual – to understand the specifics and to be able to generalise

---

9   This section draws heavily on the work of Viviane Robinson (see Robinson, 2018, 2023).

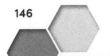

creatively about them – that makes for successful strategists. ... Remaining in the stratosphere of the conceptual is not better than having one's feet planted in concrete.

Mintzberg (2009, p. 163)

In our current context, the strategic focus could be any one of a number of intractable and complex problems – for example, persistent absence rates in one of our schools, the rising tide of adolescent mental health problems, the problem with gangs and youth violence, food and/or shelter insecurity – perhaps affecting one of our schools very acutely.

Analysing the problem

Once the strategic focus is identified, it is important to inquire into the causes and seek to understand the root causes in an analytic, no-blame way. Test rather than assume the validity of your own beliefs or assumptions about the problem. Then build a more accurate and complete picture about the causes and possible solutions. In other words, staying with the problem before looking to solutions is important. Robinson writes:

Leaders with strong analysis virtues are motivated to test rather than assume the validity of the beliefs that guide their actions and reactions. They have a high need to inquire into the facts of the matter, to understand complex problems, and to think carefully about the reasons for their decisions. They recognise the difference between knowledge and beliefs and, therefore, that what is believed to be true may be based on mistaken or incomplete understandings.

Robinson (2023, p. 127)

She goes on to observe that analytic problem-solving is a disciplined form of curiosity.

Catalysing collective leadership

I wrote at the start of this chapter that finding solutions to the complex problems that face us is unlikely to be within the reach of individual institutions. It is likely to require a collective response. Robinson reminds us that the process of forming and integrating constraints is a highly creative one (Robinson, 2023, p. 147). In the context of this work with civic partners, creativity refers to 'the production of viable or workable new, or original solutions to complex, novel ill-defined problems' (Mumford *et al.*, 2014, p. 758).

So, as we begin the work of analysing the problem, we also need to decide who else needs to be part of the conversation.

Creating and co-constructing solutions: a theory of action[10]

The analytic mind enables us to examine the problem and seek to understand its root causes. Robinson argues that it is the imaginative virtues of creativity and problem-solving that enable us to create a theory of action (Robinson, 2023, p. 147). She writes:

Imaginative virtues are critical to [this] stage of complex collaborative problem solving – the stage in which solution requirements are modified in ways that increase the possibilities for their integration. Leaders with strong imaginative virtues accept the initial uncertainty and complexity of multiple solution requirements because their past experience, their deep domain specific knowledge, and their ability to learn give them confidence that they can craft a satisfactorily integrative solution.

Robinson (2023, pp. 154–155)

A theory of action is likely to be based on these integrative solutions. It will set out what each organisation will do to bring about positive change on the issue.

A hypothetical example of what this approach could achieve

I want to apply the problem-solving approach to the rise in adolescent mental health conditions. I offer this analysis in the spirit of humility and curiosity about what could be.

- **Finding the strategic focus:** Adolescent mental ill health is a significant contributing factor to persistent absence in one school. There are very long waiting lists for the children and adolescent mental health services (CAMHS) in the local area, typically more than a year. Educational psychology services are now deployed only towards servicing statutory processes of education, health and care plans (EHCPs). There is very little community-based 'early intervention' provision in the local area.

10　I use the term 'theory of action' rather than theory of change. This is because a theory of action is more focused on a specific pathway and an organisation's role in achieving a particular change. A theory of change identifies all the processes through which change is expected to occur.

- **Analysing the problem:** Prior to 2010, the local authority commissioned some early intervention mental health services through its 'CAMHS grant'. In 2010, this grant was no longer ringfenced and put into an 'area-based grant'. Over three successive years, the area-based grant was cut from local authority settlements. The local authority in this area understandably and reluctantly had to decommission community-based provision. This put upward pressure on clinic-based services and the result was that the threshold for clinic-based services was raised. The global pandemic exacerbated adolescent mental ill health at a time when provision in the community was very limited and the upward pressure on CAMHS resulted in long waiting times.

- **Catalysing collective leadership:** You work with the council's director of children's services to invite the chief executive of the mental health trust and chief executive of the local integrated care board (ICB) to a breakfast meeting.

- **Creating and co-constructing solutions:** You learn that the 'did not attend/ was not brought' rate for the local children and young people mental health clinic is between 14% and 20%. This means that approximately one in five children and young people were not brought or did not attend their clinic appointment. This is a significant concern for the NHS mental health trust. The school in your trust with high rates of persistent absence and high rates of mental ill health is in an area where poverty is endemic. The school is two bus journeys from the clinic. The CAMHS does not routinely send reminders of appointments, which could have been made up to a year ago. You offer to create a community-based local hub in the schools to provide a 'clinic' closer to home with extended opening hours, and you all agree that a messaging service to parents will be implemented. This clinic will also be available to other children and young people in the immediate local area – not just the children in the school.

Solving the problem of high levels of children being discharged from the Child Development Centre in Feltham

Ed Vainker, chief executive of the Reach Foundation, which works in the Feltham community in West London and runs Reach Academy Feltham, noticed that some children coming into the nursery with severe needs had been discharged from the local child development centre (CDC). Furthermore, these children could not be re-referred for two years from the point of discharge.

He arranged to meet with the director of the CDC to find out a little bit more about the context for these decisions. In his conversations with the director, they talked about the challenge of parents who did not bring their children for appointments despite letters being sent to the family offering appointments. If a family missed an appointment twice, they were automatically discharged from the CDC. The director of the CDC clearly shared Ed's concern about the high levels of 'did not attend' (DNA) rates.

Working together, they planned two 'upstream' interventions. The first is that when the CDC receives a referral, it automatically copies the referring agency (usually a nursery provider) into the appointment letter to the parents. This means that the referring agency can remind the parents about the appointment – and sometimes even offer help to enable the parents to attend the appointment.

The second intervention was to bring some of the clinical resource out of the CDC and into the community one day a week – premised on the idea that the clinician could form relationships with parents and the community.

These two simple, no-cost interventions significantly reduced the DNA rate and ensured that children could receive the assessment and care they needed, and could make the best possible start at school.

A civic response to poverty

I now turn to two examples from Oasis Community Learning: a hub in one Oasis school designed to address some of the problems associated with food and shelter insecurity, and a hub in another Oasis school designed around youth violence reduction.

Oasis Community Hubs
Oasis Hub Foundry

Once known as the 'school on Benefits Street', now rated as an 'outstanding' school, Oasis Academy Foundry is part of the local community of Winson Green, Birmingham. The local neighbourhood is rich in people, diversity, talent and community spirit – alongside multiple deprivations that create daily challenges. Local community members invest their time, skills and life experience in helping one another.

The Oasis Hub Foundry team has set up food pantries that provide 1,000 meals a week, with 40 families visiting each week to access good, affordable food. Open to everyone in the community, the pantries were set up with local community members and are run by local volunteers. A clothing bank also runs alongside the food pantries, along with advice services and 'lived experience advocates', who help with everything from housing and school applications to debt, form-filling and benefits support. The team runs a toddler group and conversational English classes, as well as English for speakers of other languages and teaching assistant training courses, and offers many volunteering opportunities aimed at improving employability.

The Oasis Community Hub team has worked with two other local organisations (Warm Earth and the Newbigin Community Trust) to transform an underused school field into a community garden and event space. Many local families lived in overcrowded housing, with little access to green/outdoor space, so the community garden has become a centre for community gatherings, a source of pride in the local area, and a creative space providing room for everything from animal therapy with its own alpacas to holiday activities, food growing in polytunnels, and regular community events with up to 250 people.

The local neighbourhood is significantly impacted by poverty, evidenced by levels of pupil premium funding, families with 'no recourse to public funds' and the turnover of families in temporary accommodation. The community team provides direct and intensive support to families referred from the school, contributing to the school's contextual safeguarding as well as helping to support school attendance. The hub model means that the community team can pick up wider issues that the school (alone) doesn't have capacity for, creating 360-degree holistic care, greater stability and community cohesion.

Youth work at Oasis Hub Hadley

Oasis Academy Hadley is a high-achieving all-through academy in an area of London with high levels of serious violence affecting young people (the 10th highest in the country). The Oasis Hub model has created a community and youth team around the school, providing wraparound support for school families as well as serving the wider local community. Oasis Hub Hadley community outreach programmes provide family support, advice work, a food pantry and free café accessed by around 250 families, a baby clothes bank and toy library, and a weekly luncheon club and small groups for seniors – all delivered by staff and community volunteers.

Oasis Hub Hadley also has an extensive youth team, whose work alongside the academy both prevents and responds to serious violence. Open access and targeted group programmes run each week, as well as one-to-one mentoring. The academy is able to refer higher-risk young people to mentoring and small groups, and to support provided by a youth mental health specialist on the team. Young people are also able to self-refer, alongside attending open-access sessions. The youth service has a team of workers embedded in the nearby North Middlesex Hospital, funded as part of the London Violence Reduction Unit. This team receive referrals for any young people aged 11–24 who have attended A&E as a result of violence. The hospital-based team provides mentoring for 24–48 weeks following any incident, and typically deals with 200–250 referrals each year. The hub model provides an ecosystem of support around young people, meaning that mentoring can be accompanied by work with the wider family through the community team, as well as linking up with in-school support and response.

The mix of community, school and hospital-based work provides Oasis Hub Hadley with crucial intelligence around local issues and neighbourhood needs – including gang activity – benefiting the school's contextual safeguarding and holistic care of students, and helping preventative action. The hub model provides targeted support beyond the capacity of academy staff (alone), and provides a strong and positive local neighbourhood presence.

In this chapter, we have considered a problem orientation approach to catalysing collective leadership. The chapter has relied heavily on Viviane Robinson's work. We have considered the importance of a theory of action that can mobilise organisations around solutions to a problem, based on careful analysis of the problem. The work of the Child Development Centre at Feltham and the Oasis Community Learning Hubs provides real end-point examples of this kind of civic leadership.

References

Mintzberg, H. (2009). *Managing*. Berret-Koehler.

Mumford, M., Gibson, C., Giorgini, V. and Mecca, J. (2014). 'Leading for creativity: peoples, products and system', in D.V. Day (ed.), *The Oxford Handbook of Leadership and Organisations*, pp. 757–782. Oxford University Press.

Robinson, V. (2018). *Reduce Change to Increase Improvement*. Corwin.

Robinson, V. (2023). *Virtuous Educational Leadership: Doing the Right Work the Right Way*. Corwin.

Senge, P., Hamilton, H. and Kania, J. (2015). 'The dawn of system leadership', *Stanford Social Innovation Review*, Winter. Available at: https://ssir.org/articles/entry/the_dawn_of_system_leadership#.

CHAPTER NINE
THE PROTECTION AND PROMOTION OF PUBLIC VALUES

In this chapter and the next, I move the focus away from civic leadership defined as working with other civic actors for the wider common good, towards civic leadership as working with people and communities. I wrote in the Introduction to this book that civic leadership is different from community leadership. Community leader is a designation for a person widely perceived to represent a community. Civic leadership is about the protection and promotion of public values, and addressing issues of place or public concern. This chapter is a bit more theoretical – it seeks to understand what public value is, why it is important, how public value is created, the importance of building public trust and confidence, and the implications for leadership.

What is public value?

New Public Management has for decades dominated successive governments' approaches to managing public services. Drawing on the commercial sector, New Public Management is built on concepts like targets and choice to reform and/or drive improvements in public services.

Ben Glover, from the think tank Demos, says that New Public Management was the governing philosophy of public service reform which sought to inject private-sector managerialism into public services. Glover has published a strong analysis of why New Public Management has perhaps run its course. He argues that we have seen the effectiveness of its policy prescriptions weaken (Glover, 2024).

Glover proposes that a revolution in thinking has happened locally, which has challenged many of the key tenets of New Public Management, primarily:

- *Designing for complexity, instead of assuming the world is simple and linear.*
- *Understanding human behaviour as intrinsically motivated, rather than just responding best to external motivators, for example punishments and rewards (e.g. targets, sanctions).*

- *Building resilience to unlock prevention, not always seeking to deliver more efficiency.*
- *Experimentalism, not command and control.*

Glover (2024, p. 8)

Glover, and Demos's Future Public Services Taskforce, conclude that we need a new approach.

Prudence Brown argues that public value management has emerged as a response to the limitations of New Public Management, to incorporate notions of more democratic and inclusive dialogue and deliberation (Brown, 2021).

Public value can be defined as the value that an organisation contributes to society. The term was originally coined by Harvard professor Mark Moore at the turn of the century (Moore, 1995). Originally, public value creation was seen as the legitimate role of governments; indeed, in 2017, Sir Michael Barber wrote an influential report for then prime minister, Theresa May, on practical steps for unlocking public value (Barber, 2017). Barber proposed four pillars of a public value assessment framework for government: pursuing goals, managing inputs, engaging users and citizens, and developing system capacity.

More recently, the concept of public values has been seen to have a wider application to public organisations' contribution to the common good. Public value creation has now become a general term associated with the processes of collaborative work directed at resolving social problems and achieving shared goals or purposes.

Moore created a strategic triangle as an analytical framework (Moore, 2013). The strategic triangle is often cited as a way of understanding and measuring the public value organisations create, and what kind of capability and capacity is required to create it.

The framework asks three critical questions about the outcome of any public value exercise:

1. Does it create public value?
2. Is there legitimacy and support for the conception of public value?
3. Is there operational capacity to get it done?

These three questions create the points of the strategic triangle. The challenge for public leaders is to ensure that all three of these points are in alignment and mutually reinforcing.

Why is public value important?

In their November 2020 report, 'Democracy in dark times', Professors James Hunter, Carl Bowman and Kyle Puetz describe a slowly evolving crisis of credibility for American institutions (Hunter, Bowman and Puetz, 2020). The UK has long prided itself on the strength of its institutions, but the World Values Survey, one of the largest academic social surveys in the world, shows that the British public are not as convinced as they once were, and we are now more negative than many other countries (Duffy, 2024).

Low or declining confidence levels in our public institutions matter. The pandemic showed how much we rely on public cooperation in times of crisis, making trust in the institutions asking us to do extraordinary things crucial. The Casey Review of the Metropolitan Police emphasised how vital that confidence is to more day-to-day activities, and how badly it has been damaged, concluding that 'public consent is broken'.

Lemov and colleagues argue that loss of faith in institutions is a long-term trend, which began in the latter years of the twentieth century but has accelerated since. This creates a legitimation crisis: 'people are far less likely to accept or support decisions from an institution they don't trust' (Lemov et al., 2023, p. xxi).

The previous chief inspector, Amanda Spielman, wrote in the in the commentary to her seventh and final annual report:

The social contract that has long bound parents and schools together has been damaged. This unwritten agreement sees parents get their children to school every day and respect the school's policies and approach. In return, schools give children a good education and help prepare them for their next steps in life. It took years to build and consolidate, from when schooling first became compulsory.

Spielman (2023)

The fracturing of the social contract can be seen in the critical fall in school attendance, increase in poor behaviour and exponential rise in parental complaints. Lemov et al. argue that: 'Schools can no longer count on receiving the goodwill and trust of the parents they serve' (2023, p. xxi). They go on to say that, 'Like the nations they are part of, schools are institutions that rely on a social contract to do their work' (2023, p. xxii).

So, doing what we have always done in schools to build parental and wider public trust and confidence is not an option. We have to think differently, 'do' differently. Lemov and colleagues (2023) propose that we need to be much more purposeful and deliberative in building connection and belonging. There are many ways to do this in our schools and our trusts. Working with parents and the wider public in a collaborative way, directing our shared attention to resolving social problems and achieving shared goals or purpose is a way to rebuild trust and confidence – to rebuild the social contract.

Rebuilding the social contract

We must provide the leadership that builds belonging with one another, with our staff, with our students and families, and with our wider communities.

If we are to rebuild the social contract with parents and the wider public, we need to shift from purely *transactional* forms of engagement to *relational* engagement with parents and the wider public. In reality, this is probably a 'both/and' rather than 'either/or'. However, we do need, more explicitly and deliberately, to build relational trust. In chapter seven, I wrote that relational trust is grounded in social respect – and respectful exchanges are marked by genuinely listening to what people say and by taking these views into account in subsequent actions. This is as important when building relationships with parents as when building relationships with other civic leaders.

Lemov *et al.* (2023) write about having words that conjure things into being – the importance of a shared vocabulary for the things we want to instil. They offer insights into being more explicit about aspects of the social contract, to help rebuild trust.

When a school or trust's leadership is explicit about its purpose, then this is public and transparent. Of course, it is important that this is done respectfully with parents, because it is easier to defend decisions when you can refer back to an explicit purpose.

Let us be clear that it is hard work to renegotiate the social contract by working with parents on the shared task of educating children, and rebuilding trust in the school as a public institution. But being explicit and eloquent about purpose helps to link people – children, staff and parents – to the purpose of the organisation and the importance of education.

Belonging as a foundation for rebuilding the social contract

At our conference in 2022, we invited Owen Eastwood, author of *Belonging: The Ancient Code of Togetherness*, to give a keynote. The book is a beautiful exploration of our primal need to belong. Eastwood writes: 'To feel a sense of belonging is to feel accepted, to feel seen and to feel included by a group of people, believing that we fit in, trusting we will be protected by them. To not feel belonging is to experience the precarious and insecure sense of an outsider' (Eastwood, 2021, p. 22).

There are some worrying trends in terms of our children and young people feeling like they belong to our schools. The Pisa 2022 report for England found that pupils in England reported a significantly lower average level of satisfaction with their lives, and fewer reported they feel they belong at school than their peers across the OECD (Ingram *et al.*, 2023). These data are supported by other reports, like the 2023 Good Childhood Report, which shows trends in children's wellbeing (Children's Society, 2023). The Children's Society research seeks to understand how young people feel about different aspects of their lives. A total of 10% of the children aged 10 to 17 who completed the household survey in May and June 2023 had low wellbeing, and almost a third were unhappy with at least one specific area of their lives.

So, there is a problem to be solved here. That is why, in 2023, our annual conference theme was belonging. We created a bridge from our 2022 annual conference, at which Eastwood gave his compelling keynote, to the 2023 annual conference with the theme of belonging. We do not want our conferences to be seen as a moment in time but rather a story narrated over years about who we need to be and what we need to do to solve the challenges that face us.

We invited Doug Lemov to give the keynote in 2023, following the publication of his book (with Lewis, Williams and Frazier), *Reconnect: Building School Culture for Meaning, Purpose and Belonging* (Lemov et al., 2023). Lemov gave beautiful examples of the micro-routines of classrooms that send signals of belonging. We need to test, codify and implement the many ways in which we make sure all our children feel connected to our schools and feel like they belong.

There is something hugely powerful in saying to a child who doesn't know what it means to belong anywhere, or is unsure that they belong at all, 'I'm glad you're here. You belong here.'

The Education Endowment Foundation has published an excellent, evidence-based resource on supporting school attendance, which includes building a culture of community and belonging for pupils (Education Endowment Foundation, 2024).

There is other research evidence that demonstrates the connection between school belonging and students' motivational, social-emotional, behavioural and academic outcomes (Korpershoek *et al.*, 2020) and the impact of school-based interventions for building school belonging (Allen *et al.*, 2022).

In 2022, Teach First commissioned a team of researchers at the University of Nottingham to conduct research to address two questions: what does 'inclusion' mean to pupils, teachers and leaders, and how do relatively more inclusive secondary schools approach and practice inclusion?

The research report, called 'Belonging schools', highlights the centrality of human relationships underpinned by shared values in the six case study schools. These relationships and values created a sense of belonging – of students being seen, known, cared for, understood and supported in ways that best met their needs – from which inclusion was an outcome (Greany *et al.*, 2023).

River Learning Trust: cultures of belonging and connectedness

River Learning Trust is a trust of 28 schools (nine secondary and 19 primary), 26 in Oxfordshire and two in Swindon, plus a teaching school hub and a large school-centred initial teacher training provider. Of the 28 schools, 13 joined the trust as either inadequate or schools 'requiring improvement'. It is a diverse trust, with schools ranging in size from 100 to over 2,000 pupils, serving a wide range of communities, from 10% to 65% of pupils eligible for the pupil premium, and higher than national averages for percentages of pupils with special educational needs and disabilities (SEND).

Like most schools and trusts, challenges linked to attendance, mental health, the widened disadvantage gap post-pandemic, and the higher levels of complex SEND in schools, caused the trust to reflect on the question: for which of our pupils do our schools, and classrooms, not work … and why not? The trust's deeper exploration of connectedness and belonging gained momentum in 2022–23 stimulated by discussions with a local professor of child and adolescent psychiatry and the publication of various resources such as *Reconnect* (Lemov *et al.*, 2023), *The Kindness Principle* (Whitaker, 2021), *Motivated Teaching* (Mccrea, 2020) and *A Good Life* (Newmark and Rees, 2022).

It was reassuring and encouraging to see the national momentum building around this area and the recognition of the importance of human relationships, which perhaps was being downgraded in the wider system among a desire for clarity of process and regulation in schools; there was a risk that schools were becoming too transactional – where at their heart they are relational communities.

The trust also uses the two terms *connectedness* and *belonging*, recognising the nuance that each brings, and that starting with connection can often promote the sense of belonging we seek for our children and young people.

- Connectedness: 'Interactions where each person is heard, seen, known and valued' (Korpershoek *et al.*, 2020).
- Belonging: 'The extent to which pupils feel personally accepted, respected, included, and supported by others in the school social environment' (Goodenow and Grady, 1993).

To support its schools, the trust frames the work on connection and belonging in different areas, and is developing school-level case studies and supportive guidance. The areas are: school values and leadership; within classrooms; life outside the classroom; engagement with parents and carers; and work with external partners and the wider community.

While this reads like a list of 'what schools do', the focus is on pupils who are at risk of being most disconnected from school, as well as promoting healthy cultures where schools are inclusive by design. There is also a power in intentionality, recognising that by having a focus on what might be a normal part of school life – even as simple as the quality of greetings and conversation at the gate at the start of the day – the impact can be very significant for some pupils.

Wheatley Park School

One of the trust's secondary schools, Wheatley Park School, has focused on engaging its students with two core messages, both of which are rooted in the school's values. First, that strong teams are diverse (imagine a football team with only attackers) but united by their values (in the school's case, Everyone Learning and Everyone Caring). Therefore, at Wheatley Park, difference is actively celebrated. Second, explicitly talking about connection and belonging as a fundamental human need and building belonging by demonstrating the value of everyone caring towards each other.

This work was introduced through assemblies and regular briefings and backed up by a focus on specific ongoing habits, such as giving and receiving warm greetings, and high-profile events such as an annual student-led 'diversity day'.

Throughout it there has been a focus on disadvantaged pupils, and the attendance of this group (who typically report a weaker sense of belonging) has improved by 7%, while their persistent absence has reduced by 13% compared to the previous year.

Bayards Hill Primary School

At Bayards Hill Primary School there has been a focus on whole-school culture and pupils' belonging, to support school improvement. The school has almost 50% of pupils eligible for pupil premium and was judged 'good' by Ofsted for the first time in its history in June 2023.

A key strand of its work was the relationships between staff and children through quality first teaching and the redevelopment of the behaviour policy. The historic policy was not widely understood by staff, and they relied heavily on a behaviour support team that would provide an alternative location for students who could not regulate in the classroom. This space created a sense of otherness, and the children who were dysregulated often chose to remain there for many hours.

The school also recognised that quality first teaching was not always as strong as it needed to be to enable all pupils to be successful. As such, the school's instructional coach worked closely with the SENCO to create continuous professional development for all staff that enabled high-quality teaching for all children, especially those with SEND. The senior leadership team worked alongside the staff team to rewrite the behaviour policy, taking its key principles from Tom Sherrington and Oliver Caviglioli's WalkThrus (Sherrington and Caviglioli, 2020).

The quality, clarity and kindness developed through this work is benefiting outcomes (the school saw a significant improvement in key stage 2 results in 2024), attendance, parental confidence and staff wellbeing.

While the journey of this school could be described as typical school improvement journey, the trust is clear that doing this work through the lens of creating a culture of connectedness and belonging has been motivating and meaningful for staff, as well as impactful for pupils, creating positive relationships which will sustain the journey of improvement.

Remaking relationships

Building connection and belonging may mean that we need to remake and reframe relationships – we may need to build on forms of transaction engagement with relational engagement.

Hilary Cottam writes:

Relationships – the simple human bonds between us – are the foundation of good lives. They bring us joy, happiness and a sense of possibility. And they are what Martha Nussbaum calls 'architectonic'. Building on relationships enables the growth of further capability: supporting us to learn, contributing to good health and vibrant communities. Without strong bonds with others, or with unhealthy relationships, very few of us can feel fulfilled – or even function.

Cottam (2018)

At times of crisis, when parents and school staff need to work together in difficult circumstances in the best interests of children, a strong relationship makes this much more likely to be successful. It is helpful to build on an existing relationship rather than to encounter someone for the first time when things are difficult. When we think about the text messages we send to parents, should we consider whether we are communicating in a purely transactional way, or using the opportunity to build a relationship? When a child returns on a Monday after having missed school on a Friday for no discernible reason, how do we greet that child in a way that encourages this week to be 100% attendance?

Cottam reflects that we must design ways to encounter each other if we are to flourish, because 'relationships sit at the heart of a good life, and our capacity to relate to one another is infinite' (Cottam, 2018, p. 207).

Community organising

One of the ways to create public value, rebuild the social contract and remake relationships is through the concept of community organising. In the case study below, Dr Seb Chapleau outlines how an increasing number of trusts are embracing the methods of community organising across England.

Dr Chapleau argues that at the heart of community organising is a deep belief in the importance of civil society and its institutions: those institutions dotted across our neighbourhoods that, for hundreds of years, have shaped the lives of our communities. These include religious institutions and community organisations, which have taught – implicitly or explicitly – many people about the importance of coming together; youth groups, where many have learned to navigate through friendships and arguments; and voluntary organisations, where people have learned to manoeuvre through an eclectic range of connections that can teach a great deal about the meaning of life.

In this case study, Dr Chapleau introduces the concept of 'anchor institutions'. This is the subject of the next chapter.

Community Organising
By Dr Seb Chapleau, assistant director at Citizens UK

Civil society is the backbone of a strong community, where relationality is key and social capital is built. Anchor institutions are essential to maintaining this notion of social capital. These institutions serve a purpose that transcends their immediate outcomes: a nursery isn't just about childcare, a school isn't simply there to teach academic skills, and a local football club isn't merely there to entertain for 90 minutes. As anchor institutions, these places intrinsically serve a greater purpose by creating links between people and sustaining the social capital that gives life meaning.

The decline of civil society, as noted by Robert Putnam in his seminal *Bowling Alone* (Putnam, 2001), is concerning. Weaker links between people, community fragmentation and increasing individualism lead to a lack of trust and solidarity. What is noticeable at a neighbourhood level – where fewer people know or interact with their neighbours – has an impact at local and international levels. 'Stranger danger' now oddly characterises societal evolution.

With this decline in social capital, some trusts have embraced their civic role to reverse the trend. While the primary role of a school is to educate young people, more trusts are building relationships to challenge structures impacting learning and wellbeing.

One reason some trusts engage with issues in their communities is that many of the public services that used to support families are no longer available. The fabric of the welfare state has been eroding over the past 15–20 years, and schools have increasingly played roles other services once did. The Covid-19 pandemic highlighted this issue. Another reason is that many issues schools face, such as attainment, attendance and wellbeing, stem from societal problems. Unless addressed upstream, school leaders cannot resolve these problems. Simply extending the school day or adding more revision sessions will not address the root causes.

Some schools and trusts have therefore engaged with community organising to address social problems impacting students.

Take St Thomas More Catholic High School in North Shields, part of the Bishop Bewick Catholic Education Trust. Addressing mental health challenges faced by students has been a key priority. Employing in-house counsellors was unsustainable due to shrinking budgets. Through Tyne and Wear Citizens, a local alliance of civil society organisations, St Thomas More developed a plan to hold local politicians accountable. The collaboration led to a regional government-funded pilot programme for school-based counsellors. In April 2024, further agreements from Mayor Kim McGuinness were secured to deploy counsellors across all secondary schools in the region.

Surrey Square Primary School in Southwark, London, part of the Big Education Trust, faces considerable housing pressures. Situated on the Aylesbury Estate, one of Europe's largest housing estates, families at Surrey Square have dealt with squalid conditions, rising rents and gentrification. Leaders at Surrey Square, through Southwark Citizens, have been working to hold their local council accountable, addressing pressures affecting student attainment, attendance and wellbeing. Community meetings involving families, teachers and local community members have led to strategies holding decision-makers accountable. As a result, solutions have been developed, and some of the issues too many young people experience – lack of sleep, lack of space to do homework, etc. – are being addressed and resolved.

Finally, consider the work of Co-op Academies Trust, Dixons Academies Trust, Beckfoot Trust, Bradford Diocesan Academies Trust, Exceed Academies Trust and Priestley Academy Trust, which have come together to build Bradford Citizens. Working together across Bradford, these trusts have trained hundreds of staff, young people and families to take action on the issues that too often tarnish their city and impact young people's achievement and wellbeing.

All in all, community organising is used by an increasing number of trusts and schools to find practical ways to reweave the fabric of civil society, the very fabric we all need to live more cohesive and meaningful lives. Beyond the wish to strengthen relationships between institutions, what community organising provides trust leaders with is a set of tools and strategies to challenge the structural and societal inequities too many young people and their families face across our neighbourhoods. It provides trust leaders with tools that enable them to embrace their civic responsibility and work across the infrastructure that shapes the way young people grow and, hopefully, thrive.

I want to conclude this section with a beautiful concept from the land of my birth – that of 'Ubuntu'. In 2006, Nelson Mandela gave us his explanation of Ubuntu, in an interview with South African journalist Tim Modise:

A traveller through a country would stop at a village and he didn't have to ask for food or for water. Once he stops, the people give him food, entertain him. That is one aspect of Ubuntu, but it will have various aspects. Ubuntu does not mean that people should not enrich themselves. The question therefore is: Are you going to do so in order to enable the community around you to be able to improve?

Mandela (2006)

Ubuntu means a quality that includes the essential human virtues of compassion and humanity, but it also means 'I am because we are.' It is the profound sense that we are human only through the humanity of others.

In this time of social, economic and political challenge, when people have lost faith in institutions, we must exemplify the standards of public life. We must build school cultures where our children, parents, staff and wider community feel like they belong.

References

Allen, K.A., Jamshidi, N., Berger, E. *et al.* (2022). 'Impact of school-based interventions for building school belonging in adolescence: a systematic review', *Educational Psychology Review*, 34, 229–257. Available at: https://link.springer.com/article/10.1007/s10648-021-09621-w#citeas.

Barber, M. (2017). *Delivering better outcomes for citizens: practical steps for unlocking public value*. Independent report led by Sir Michael Barber. HM Treasury. Available at: https://www.gov.uk/government/publications/delivering-better-outcomes-for-citizens-practical-steps-for-unlocking-public-value.

Brown, P.R. (2021). 'Public value measurement vs. public value creating imagination: the constraining influence of old and new public management paradigms', *International Journal of Public Administration*, 44(10), 808–817.

Children's Society (2023). *The good childhood report 2023*. Available at: https://www.childrenssociety.org.uk/information/professionals/resources/good-childhood-report-2023.

Cottam, H. (2018). *Radical Help: How We Can Remake the Relationships Between Us and Revolutionise the Welfare State*. Virago.

Duffy, B. (2024). *How the UK lost confidence in its institutions*. Available at: https://www.uk-values.org/news-comment/how-the-uk-lost-confidence-in-its-institutions.

Eastwood, O. (2021). *Belonging: The Ancient Code of Togetherness*. Quercus.

Education Endowment Foundation (2024). *Supporting school attendance*. Available at: https://educationendowmentfoundation.org.uk/education-evidence/leadership-and-planning/supporting-attendance.

Glover, B. (2024). *Liberated public services: a new vision for citizens, professionals and policy makers*. Demos. Available at: https://demos.co.uk/wp-content/uploads/2024/05/Taskforce-Vision-Paper_May.pdf.

Goodenow, C. and Grady, K. (1993). 'The relationship of school belonging and friends' values to academic motivation among urban adolescent students', *Journal of Experimental Education*, 62(1), 60–71.

Greany, T., Pennacchia, J., Graham, J. and Bernardes, E. (2023). *Belonging schools: how do relatively more inclusive secondary schools approach and practise inclusion?* Teach First. Available at: https://www.teachfirst.org.uk/belonging-schools.

Hunter, J.D., Bowman, C.D. and Puetz, K. (2020). *Democracy in dark times*. Available at: https://iasculture.org/research/publications/democracy-in-dark-times.

Ingram, J., Stiff, J., Cadwallader, S., Lee, G. and Kayton, H. (2023). *Pisa 2022: national report for England*. Government Social Research. Available at: https://www.gov.uk/government/publications/pisa-2022-national-report-for-england.

Korpershoek, H., Canrinus, E., Fokkens-Bruinsma, M. and De Boer, H. (2020). 'The relationships between school belonging and students' motivational, social-emotional, behavioural, and academic outcomes in secondary education: a meta-analytic review', *Research Papers in Education*, 35(6), 641–680.

Lemov, D., Lewis, H., Williams, D. and Frazier, D. (2023). *Reconnect: Building School Culture for Meaning, Purpose, and Belonging*. Jossey Bass.

Mandela, N. (2006). *Experience Ubuntu*. Interview with Tim Modise (audio/video file), 24 May. Available at: https://en.wikipedia.org/wiki/File:Experience_ubuntu.ogv.

Mccrea, P. (2020). *Motivated Teaching: Harnessing the Science of Motivation to Boost Attention and Effort in the Classroom*. CreateSpace Independent Publishing Platform.

Moore, M. (1995). *Creating Public Value: Strategic Management in Government*. Harvard University Press.

Moore, M. (2013). *Recognizing Public Value*. Harvard University Press.

Newmark, B. and Rees, T. (2022). *A good life: towards greater dignity for people with learning disability*. CST and Ambition Institute. Available at: https://cstuk.org.uk/knowledge/guidance-and-policy/a-good-life-towards-greater-dignity-for-people-with-learning-disability/.

Putnam, R. (2001). *Bowling Alone: The Collapse and Revival of American Community*. Simon & Schuster.

Sherrington, T. and Caviglioli, O. (2020). *Teaching WalkThrus: Five-step Guides to Instructional Coaching: Visual Step-by-step Guides to Essential Teaching Techniques*. John Catt.

Spielman, A. (2023). 'HMCI commentary', *Annual Report of His Majesty's Chief Inspector of Education, Children's Services and Skills 2022/23*. HM Government. Available at: https://www.gov.uk/government/publications/ofsted-annual-report-202223-education-childrens-services-and-skills/the-annual-report-of-his-majestys-chief-inspector-of-education-childrens-services-and-skills-202223.

Whitaker, D. (2021). *The Kindness Principle: Making Relational Behaviour Management Work in Schools*. Independent Thinking Press.

CHAPTER TEN
COMMUNITY ANCHORING

By James Townsend, Ed Vainker and Leora Cruddas

This chapter continues the focus on civic leadership as working with people and communities. The concept of the trust as an anchor institution is explored. Anchor institutions, alongside their main purpose, play a significant role in a locality by making a strategic contribution to the greater social good. We want to acknowledge at the outset that schools have always worked with society in different ways, and most have always been at the centre of their communities. The naming of school trusts as 'anchor institutions' is about a rebalance away from a very centralised education system towards something that is much more located in communities. It is an explicit commitment to building trusts not as corporate structures that dislocate schools from their communities but as helping schools to be ever more located in the communities they serve. It helps us to think about trusts as public institutions, civic in their outlook, anchored in their communities.

This chapter is a lightly edited version of a paper published with the Reach Foundation. It is considered jointly authored with James Townsend and Ed Vainker (Townsend, Vainker and Cruddas, 2023).

What is an anchor institution?

As school trusts emerge as civic structures, there is an opportunity for them to be anchor institutions in their communities. Typically anchor institutions:

- have strong ties to the geographic area in which they are based
- tend to be larger employers and have significant purchasing power
- are public sector, not-for-profit or, as in the case of school trusts, charitable organisations
- tend to receive (or are significant stewards of) public resources.

The idea of anchor institutions is not new. The concept originated in the United States in the 1960s. By the turn of the century, urban universities felt that they could no longer ignore the conditions their communities were experiencing. As a consequence, universities started to create partnerships with other local and civic organisations to address the complex social and economic challenges faced by their local communities.

The challenges we face currently are daunting: global political and economic uncertainty, the rise in child poverty and destitution, pressures on public services, the continuing impacts of Covid-19 and the climate emergency, to name but a few. These are challenges we cannot address on our own. Great schools are necessary but not sufficient if we are to enable all children to enjoy lives of choice and opportunity.

An 'anchor institution' is an organisation with an important presence in a place. In England, NHS trusts (Reed *et al.*, 2019) and universities (Civic University Network, 2018) have arguably been more conscious of their role as anchors. While many trusts already do important work in ensuring all children can access full opportunities offered by schools, we argue that seeing trusts as 'anchor institutions' opens up longer time frames and broadens our thinking about how we best address our collective mission to advance education.

What makes a school trust a strong community anchor?

In this section, we develop our thinking about the opportunities that school trusts have as anchor institutions. While they will share features with other anchor institutions, such as NHS trusts or universities (discussed above), we describe here the *particular* benefit of school trusts acting as anchor institutions. We argue there are three features of school trusts that – if maximised – will allow them to be particularly effective community anchor institutions.

School trusts have long-lasting relationships with children and families

School trusts have relationships with families that may last for up to twenty years. No other public institution has such long-lasting relationships with so many families. Other public services, such as the NHS, are also universal, but no others see all children every day. This presents a unique opportunity for trusts to act as anchor institutions.

By orienting to the long term and investing in relationships with children and families, possibilities open up for trusts as anchor institutions. Long-lasting, trusting relationships enable trusts to build strong alignment with families on how best to support their children's education, enable early identification of children and families that require additional support, and provide children and families with stable support in times of challenge. When combined with strong alignment with other professionals who may be supporting children and families at different points in their lives, these long-standing relationships are, indeed, 'anchoring'.

Long-lasting relationships enable us to think broadly about outcomes we want for children

Great schools are necessary but not sufficient if all children are to enjoy lives of choice and opportunity. There is no doubt that academic outcomes are hugely important to children's futures. These are rightly prioritised by school trusts, and we are rightly held accountable for these outcomes by the government.

But rather than accountability being perceived as something that is *only* externally imposed by the government, we could shift it in the direction of trust boards being ever more explicit and eloquent about *their* vision, *their* 'theory of change' and *their* measures that will evidence success. The measures will need to include the government's performance measures but need not be constrained by them.

In other words, we must move to measuring what we value in our school, or group of schools, and our communities. In local trusts, this is likely to be one unified theory of change; in other, more geographically dispersed trusts, it will require local clusters or individual schools developing their own community vision underneath an overarching trust vision. In all cases, if duly invested in, the long-lasting relationships we have with children and families provide a strong foundation on which to build a compelling theory of change.

Trusts as anchor institutions can harness professional accountability to the children and communities we serve (Cruddas, 2021). How we articulate the measures that are important to us, in addition to (not instead of) the state's performance measures, is core to each trust's education philosophy. Trusts could consider through a visioning process:

- What do we mean by advancing education?
- What do we care about?
- What matters to our communities?
- What do we promise to our communities?

Answering these questions with precision and specificity means that parents and communities can be invited to hold the trust to account for these, in addition to the academic outcomes of education.

To be clear, we are not suggesting trusts should deliver many or all services. Rather, we should ask ourselves, what can we do to support achievement of the broad outcomes we desire for children, especially those experiencing economic disadvantage? To be an anchor institution means thinking and acting strategically and in partnership to meet our broader goals for our children. This requires a deep understanding of children's lives and of the communities we serve, and strong relationships with other civic actors. Without this strategic lens, there is a risk that our 'community work' will be piecemeal and low impact. If we harness the power of agency as interdependence – a collective effort to secure good outcomes – alongside a shift in our accountability system towards internal ownership, we may finally have the conditions in which all children, regardless of background, can access the support they need to thrive.

School and trusts leaders' moral purpose – we can build on this in developing civic leadership

The moral purpose of our school and trust leaders is one of the defining characteristics of our system. We are yet to meet a school or trust leader who does not care deeply about the children in their care. The willingness to go – when needed – 'beyond the call of duty' in the support we provide our children and families is a huge strength. As with long-lasting relationships and professional accountability for outcomes, our collective moral purpose is a hugely valuable asset as an anchor institution. As our moral purpose drives our educational ambitions, so it can drive our wider civic role as well.

So, we need trust leaders who are strategic builders of local and regional systems, and who can build partnerships and ways of working that harness the moral purpose of teachers and others working with children and families. As leaders of groups of schools, trust leaders *already* seek to maximise the benefit of multiple organisations working together. Anchor trusts will extend this strategic collaboration beyond their own schools to include a wider set of partners.

In this regard, we can learn from the practices of other charitable organisations and leaders that have created outsized impact. In *Forces for Good: The Six Practices of High Impact Nonprofits*, Crutchfield and McCleod Grant (2007) analyse the practices of charitable organisations that have had a significant impact on their mission. Crucially, these organisations focus both on high-quality delivery *and* on broader advocacy and partnership. The success they seek goes beyond their own organisation and instead focuses on broader outcomes or systemic change.

Leadership of trusts as 'anchor institutions'

Anchor trusts do this ...	... not this
Build and nurture strategic partnerships with other schools and other sectors supporting children and families locally.	Focus exclusively on their own organisation.
Use their position as trusted, visible institutions to improve local systems and increase their impact.	Use only organisational growth to scale their impact.
Run great schools and advocate for (local and national) policy change when needed to achieve long-term goals.	Focus only on their own schools.
Deliberately empower others (including people outside the trust) to lead and take action to support children and families.	Maintain a command-and-control hierarchy.
Invest in developing their workforce (especially locally) and contributing to strong communities.	Neglect building the workforce required for a long-term strengthening of community.
Focus on impact, and measure progress against broad outcomes for all children in communities in which the trust works.	Focus only on a narrow set of outcomes defined externally.

Source: Adapted from Crutchfield and McCleod Grant (2007)

As trusts further strengthen and as we develop our collective capacity for leading change beyond what was possible as individual schools, there is a significant opportunity to shape the next stage of our growth, so we deliver outstanding academic outcomes *and* act as anchor institutions to achieve broader outcomes for *all* children.

How do we move towards this new paradigm of community anchoring?

In the previous section, we argued that school trusts have three particular strengths as anchor institutions: uniquely long-lasting relationships with children and families; the capacity to define a compelling vision for our children and our own theory for how we will achieve that vision; and a collective moral purpose that can be harnessed for deeper impact.

In this section, we turn our attention to three ways we might start to move towards this new paradigm of community anchoring. This list is by no means exhaustive, but we hope it provides a useful starting point for colleagues considering the role of their trusts as civic institutions.

Develop a deep understanding of their communities and work closely with them

To be effective as anchor institutions, we need to know our communities really well. If we are to make the best use of our position as a universal service, we must understand the concerns, difficulties, joys and hopes of our children and the adults caring for them. We can begin to build this understanding through collecting and making use of a wider range of data than might currently be typical as school trusts. Understanding, for example, how children's postcodes correlate with their attainment, or how their attendance has changed across primary and secondary school, opens up new perspectives on how best to support those children.

We can strengthen our understanding by *mapping* our communities and their assets, building an increasingly sophisticated awareness of the location and roles that other schools, places of worship, health centres, playing fields, community centres, charities, shopping centres and parks play in the lives of our children and families. Through this mapping we can identify potential partner organisations as well as gain insights to support our mission.

Finally, we need to listen. A really deep understanding can only be gained through strong relationships with the other professionals who work with children and a clear common cause with families. Through listening campaigns that deepen our connection to our communities we not only build our understanding, we also strengthen relationships, and build the power of children, parents and members of the wider community to advance education and collectively strengthen our communities. As Hillary Cottam argues, we need to grow the capabilities of our communities: 'We can no longer invest in social systems that are designed to fix us, allocating support according to the extent we have broken down (a difficult and expensive task). Humans are designed to grow, heal when necessary and to continually develop' (Cottam, 2020). This starts with listening.

The Cradle-to-Career Partnership

The Reach Foundation convenes a national network of locally rooted schools and trusts establishing effective place-based models of 'cradle to career' support in their own communities.[11]

This is its theory of change:

> While we know exactly what every child needs to thrive, we also know that we are not securing these conditions for every child in England right now.
>
> To change this – to secure a life of choice and opportunity for every child – we believe that great schools are necessary but not sufficient.
>
> We believe that while schools and trusts have an integral role to play in securing lives of choice and opportunity for every child – they cannot do so in isolation.
>
> The national network of Cradle-to-Career Partners are working together to design, develop and deliver place-based models of 'cradle to career' support in their own communities. New models and signs of deeper integration into communities are starting to emerge.

Contribute to a coherent education experience for all children and young people

For many trusts, a starting point for moving towards being an anchor institution will be to ensure they are contributing to a coherent education experience for all children and young people, from birth to 18. As well as maximising the benefit of long-term relationships with families (as discussed above) we think there are three areas in which school trusts can work with and beyond their own organisations to ensure a coherent experience for children and families. There are, of course, many ways to do this and excellent collaboration is already underway in many communities. As anchor institutions, we believe this work is core.

- **Ensure *all* children access high-quality support from 0–5:** A total of 90% of brain development happens before the age of five. By the time children start primary school, the 'disadvantage gap' is already an

---

11   Access the website of the Cradle-to-Career Partnership here: https://www.cradletocareer.uk/.

average of 4.5 months. To make a difference to children's long-term social and educational development, trusts considering their strategic role as anchor institutions must, we think, think carefully about the opportunity to support children's experiences in the early years. This could be through, for example, developing their own nursery provision, working closely to support the professional development of early years professionals locally, or through supporting families to access high-quality provision.

- **A curriculum that is coherently sequenced and builds cumulatively:** Too many children experience a disjointed curriculum, both within and between phases of their education. This is a particular problem for pupils from economically disadvantaged backgrounds. As anchor institutions, trusts have an opportunity to reach out to schools within and beyond their trusts to backward plan and align curriculum sequences across ages and phases. Doing this will enable children to gain increasingly sophisticated disciplinary knowledge of each subject, remember large amounts of substantive knowledge, and apply and transfer their knowledge within and between subjects. For all teachers, this will enable a stronger understanding of pupils' prior knowledge, a clear understanding of what pupils will need to achieve in their subject, and stronger relationships with colleagues in different phases.

- **Excellent teaching across the phases:** Too many teachers receive poor-quality and fragmented professional development, which does not improve their teaching or pupil outcomes. As anchor institutions, trusts can consider how to develop all local teachers' knowledge and practice to improve outcomes for all children, but especially those most economically disadvantaged. Trusts thinking and supporting beyond their own organisations in developing teachers can help to ensure that children receive high-quality teaching in every lesson, resulting in greater progress, have gaps in knowledge and skills identified and closed earlier, and have increased opportunities in pursuing education and training at each transition point of school and beyond. For teachers, the benefit is a clearer shared understanding of what excellence looks like in their school/s; effective, individualised professional development and, as a result, greater motivation and an increased likelihood of staying in the profession.

Consciously develop your local workforce – the trust as an employer

School trusts are sometimes relatively large employers in their communities. Trusts should be employers of choice, offering good working conditions, paying attention to wellbeing and offering career progression. Building a workforce that is more diverse and representative of the local area can also better anchor a trust in its communities, while strengthening the community by supporting more residents into quality work.

There is an opportunity, especially in the current climate of staff shortages, for trusts to think long term about a pipeline for development into key roles. For instance, building a pathway of apprenticeships into roles across schools, and using foundation degrees and other mechanisms to help local people to grow and develop, can enrich trusts with staff who understand 'how we do things' and have important lived experience and understanding of the community.

The Reach Foundation and Kingston University Early Years Foundation Degree

Recognising the importance of all children having the best possible start in life, Reach partnered with Kingston University to create an Early Years Foundation Degree. Specifically designed for early years practitioners in Feltham (following a focused listening campaign and co-design process), the degree is taught locally and deliberately builds a strong peer network of early years professionals. Reach Academy staff benefit alongside colleagues from all other local early years settings.

'Anchor' workforce strategies can also help trusts to be better employers. The trust can act as an anchor by supporting the wellbeing of its staff through good employment conditions and the working environment. This is timely given the huge workforce supply pressures we face as a sector.

Alongside an anchor role around workforce, there is similar opportunity for trusts as commissioners of social value. Trusts have significant purchasing power. Procuring and commissioning more goods and services from local small and medium-sized enterprises (SMEs) can have an important economic impact. By spending more resources within the community, trusts as anchor organisations may help local businesses to grow, employ more people and pay higher wages, thereby stimulating local economic development.

The role of governance in enabling trusts to be anchor institutions

Trusts are complex, dynamic organisations and the governance of trusts is equally complex. In this section, we argue that the concepts of community anchoring and engagement are key to good governance.

In chapter four, the Institute on Governance's definition of good governance was used to explore four key dimensions:

1. Who has power?
2. Who makes decisions?
3. How do stakeholders make their voices heard?
4. How is account rendered?

How we answer these questions is key to successful governance of school trusts. It is clear that the authority is invested in the board by the Secretary of State under the trust's funding agreement. It is the board, ultimately, that makes decisions. The chief executive and executive team have authority and power to make decisions because the board delegates these to them. This is also true for the local tier of governance.

In answering questions three and four, we must interrogate the extent to which it is possible for trusts to further their purpose for public benefit without a deep understanding of our communities or consideration of *all* the factors influencing children's ability to flourish – especially those experiencing economic disadvantage. This is a technical requirement as well as a moral imperative:

The Charity Commission's guidance Public Benefit: Running a Charity states that when making decisions about how to carry out your charity's purpose for the public benefit you should:

- *know who can potentially benefit from your charity's purpose; and*
- *consider the full range of ways in which you could carry out your charity's purpose.*

(Cruddas, 2022)

Local governance has not historically been well defined in the trust sector. Because there is sometimes a tendency to bring the mental model of maintained school governance into the trust sector, the roles and responsibilities of local governance are sometimes muddled with maintained school governing boards. The trust board is the statutory governance board, which delegates to the local tier of governance the roles and responsibilities the trust board wishes them to perform.

We argue that local governing bodies should have specific responsibility for ensuring depth of understanding of the community and holding schools to account for using that understanding to enable children to flourish.

Whatever the constitution of the local tier, there is more that can be done to use the local tier of governance more explicitly for the purposes of community anchoring. For the avoidance of doubt, we are not advising that the local tier of governance should have *only* this function, but rather that there is enormous potential in mobilising local governance for the purposes of community anchoring.

One thing that trust boards can consider is writing explicitly into the terms of reference for the local tier of governance a responsibility for meaningful engagement with parents and local communities. The trust board can then receive expert intelligence and advice from the local tier on the things that matter most to parents and communities. In this way, the local tier of governance can be a useful way for the board to challenge its own assumptions, but also to anchor the school explicitly in its community.

However, it is probably not sufficient simply to write parent and community engagement into local terms of reference without the trust also being explicit as to what this means. We need a more strategic approach to community engagement and participation. There is a literature on community engagement that can help trusts determine how they want to engage and about what. It may be helpful for trust boards to codify this so that everyone is clear about what this means in the context of the organisation.

Below is a table that has been lightly adapted for the trust sector, drawing on the Framework of the International Association for Public Participation. Over time, a trust could seek to move along this continuum towards greater community involvement, and collaboration may evolve. While community engagement may be achieved during a time-limited project, it can involve – and often evolve into – long-term partnerships that move from the traditional focus on a single educational issue to address a range of social, economic, political and environmental factors that affect education.

Spectrum of public participation					
	Outreach	Consult	Involve	Collaborate	Empower
Public Participation Goal	To provide our community with balanced and objective information to assist them in understanding the problem, alternatives, opportunities and/or solutions.	To obtain public feedback on analysis, alternatives and/or decisions.	To work directly with our communities throughout the process to ensure that their concerns and aspirations are consistently understood and considered.	To partner with our communities in each aspect of the decision, including the development of alternatives and the identification of the preferred solution.	To place decision-making on an issue in the hands of the community.
Promise to the public	We will keep you informed.	We will keep you informed, listen to and acknowledge concerns and aspirations, and provide feedback on how your input influenced the decision.	We will work with you to ensure that your concerns and aspirations are directly reflected in the alternatives developed, and provide feedback on how you influenced the decision.	We will look to you for advice and innovation in formulating solutions, and incorporate your advice and recommendations into the decisions to the maximum extent possible.	We will implement what you decide on this issue.

Source: Adapted from IAP2 (2018)

The trust could use this framework to write into its strategy the *specific issues* – and then reach out to the community, consult, involve, collaborate or seek to empower the community. This then provides a mandate for the local tier of governance in respect of the specific issues and how the board is expecting engagement and participation to take place.

Conclusion: consciously adopting an anchor mindset

This chapter is both an invitation and a call to action. As we said in the introduction, as school trusts emerge as civic structures, we see an opportunity for them to be anchor institutions in their communities. Anchor institutions, alongside their main educational purpose, play a significant role in a locality by making a strategic contribution to the greater social good, and prioritise support for those experiencing economic disadvantage. For us, this is a social justice issue.

We want to address the issue of an external focus as potentially detracting from the core business of advancing education. We are explicitly *not* making the case that schools should be all things or that high educational standards can be compromised by a wider focus. The focus on the core business of schools as advancing education is essential and the first task of leaders is to ensure the quality of education.

We understand that, in reality, time and resources are finite. But if we are truly going to address the multiple impacts of disadvantage and narrow or eliminate the disadvantage gap, then we believe trust leaders must work with others to advance education as a wider common good. Civic trusts acting as anchor institutions in their communities create the conditions for purposeful collaboration with other schools and with civic organisations.

We believe that this kind of leadership and institutional focus is needed – school trusts must consciously adopt an anchor mindset if we are to address the multiple challenges we face in our communities, in our nation as a whole and globally.

References

Civic University Network (2018). Launched from the 2018 UPP Foundation report, *Truly civic: strengthening the connection between universities and their places*. Available at: https://www.upp-foundation.org/wp-content/uploads/2019/02/Civic-University-Commission-Final-Report.pdf.

Cottam, H. (2020). *Welfare 5.0: why we need a social revolution and how to make it happen*. Institute for Innovation and Public Purpose. Available at: https://www.ucl.ac.uk/bartlett/public-purpose/sites/public-purpose/files/iipp_welfare-state-5.0-report_hilary-cottam_wp-2020-10_final.pdf.

Cruddas, L. (2021). *Intelligent systems of accountability*, CST. Available at: https://cstuk.org.uk/knowledge/guidance-and-policy/intelligent-systems-of-accountability/.

Cruddas, L. (2022). *Public benefit and civic duty – guidance for school trusts*. CST [member-only content].

Crutchfield, L. and McCleod Grant, H. (2007). *Forces for Good: The Six Practices of High-Impact Nonprofits*. Jossey Bass.

IAP2 (2018). 'Spectrum of public participation' (table). Available at: https://cdn.ymaws.com/www.iap2.org/resource/resmgr/pillars/Spectrum_8.5x11_Print.pdf.

Reach Foundation (n.d.). *The Reach Foundation's Cradle-to-Career Partnership*. Available at: https://www.cradletocareer.uk/.

Reed, S., Göpfert, A., Wood, S., Allwood, D. and Warburton, W. (2019). *Building healthier communities: the role of the NHS as an anchor institution*. The Health Foundation. Available at: https://www.health.org.uk/publications/reports/building-healthier-communities-role-of-nhs-as-anchor-institution.

Townsend, J., Vainker, E. and Cruddas, L. (2023). *Community anchoring: school trusts as anchor institutions*. CST. Available at: https://cstuk.org.uk/knowledge/guidance-and-policy/community-anchoring-school-trusts-as-anchor-institutions/.

PART 3
SYSTEM LEADERSHIP

Chapter 11:   Building the narrative: why a trust-led system? 185

Chapter 12:   System building: acting *on*, rather than just acting *in*
the system 195

Chapter 13:   Curating the pipeline of the next generation of leaders 208

Chapter 14:   Creating the conditions for the system to keep getting better...217

Chapter 15:   Building public institutions 230

CHAPTER ELEVEN
BUILDING THE NARRATIVE: WHY A TRUST-LED SYSTEM?

As distinct from some of the legacy thinking on system or 'systems' leadership that appears to focus narrowly on the attributes of the leader, our definition of system leadership is about *system building*. Much of the literature of system leadership actually falls into what I would term civic leadership – working across professional boundaries with other civic leaders. This was the focus of the second part of this book.

In the Introduction to this book I cited Michael Fullan and Joanne Quinn's definition of 'systemness' (Fullan and Quinn, 2015). What Fullan and Quinn mean by this is focusing direction, and the need to integrate what the system is doing. Right now, in England, the system is building groups of schools.

We should work together now to build the resilience of our school system to invite all schools to join a group of schools working together in a trust.

The system leader is a strategic builder of local and regional systems. For some local school systems, we are close to an end state in terms of all schools being part of a group. In other local school systems, we are far away from this point. Trust leaders, along with regulators, must now think deliberately and intentionally about how to build local school systems.

This requires leaders who act collectively and strategically *on* – not just *in* – the system. This is the subject of the third and final section of this book. To return to Fullan and Quinn, we should build system coherence. We should not wait for governments to do this. We can do this by the power of our argument. We can be the system architects.

This chapter sets out one argument – one story if you will – for why a trust-based system is our best bet. Starting with a clear narrative is important to the task of system building. It is based on a pamphlet I wrote over the Christmas period in 2022 and which we published in 2023 (Cruddas, 2023). We launched the pamphlet at a House of Lords reception in the spring of 2023. In my speech at this event, I said:

> In these difficult times of upheaval and uncertainty, it is up to us to
> build a resilient school system that has the capacity and can create the

conditions to keep getting better. I believe that is the potential of a trust-based system.

It is over to us. It is our leadership that will prevail.

Starting with why

In chapter one, I reflected on Simon Sinek's *Start with Why* as a powerful way to lead with purpose (Sinek, 2009). His hypothesis is that those organisations that start with why are most successful because they are purpose-led. So why do I believe that a trust-based system might be our best bet for a school system that keeps on getting better?

My belief is definitely not based in the policy or ideology of any political party. And I do not believe that we should use the blunt instrument of legislative compulsion to force all schools to join a trust.

It is essential that those who lead and govern our schools believe they are making good educational decisions, based on what is best for children, young people and communities, our staff and our schools. So, we need to make the powerful case for a group of schools working together in a single legal entity.

For me, this starts with something I heard Steve Munby, formerly chief executive of the National College for School Leadership, say in 2017. He gave a speech (reproduced in Munby, 2019, p. 225) on ethical leadership in which he argued that the wrong question is, 'Should my school become an academy?' He said a much better question is, 'How can my school best collaborate with others in a strong and resilient structure to ensure that each child is a powerful learner and that adults have the opportunities to learn and develop as teachers and leaders?'

I have always thought that there is something fundamentally important and powerful in these words. A group of schools working together in a school trust is so much more than simply the changing of the legal structure of the school.

I think this starts with purpose. I am cautious to claim that I write from moral purpose because I think morality is a complex ethical and philosophical field – and there is much over-claiming of moral purpose to seek a high ground. I am saying, simply, that I think contemplating Steve Munby's beautiful question connects us to purpose – to our why.

Deep and purposeful collaboration

The first part of Munby's powerful question relates to collaboration and, by implication, purpose. Deep and purposeful collaboration is at the heart of the trust structure. And, from my point of view, structures are in fact very important because they create the conditions for this intensely focused collaboration.

There are undoubtedly other forms of inter-school collaboration, but none of them – not even the hard federation – can create quite the depth and tightness of collaboration described by David Hargreaves in his distinction between 'shallow, loose' partnership and 'tight, deep' partnership, which he described as inter-school integration (Hargreaves, 2012).

I believe that this comes primarily from the power of purpose – the capacity to link people through a shared belief about the identify, meaning and mission of an organisation. In the strongest trusts, there is a deep sense of collective purpose.

The closest expression of inter-school integration is the school trust – a group of schools working in deep and purposeful collaboration as one entity, under a single governance structure, to improve and maintain high educational standards across the group.

In my view, deep and purposeful collaboration is at the heart of the trust structure.

In 2015, the cross-party House of Commons Education Select Committee published a report on 'Academies and Free Schools', which said: 'Primary heads told us that, whilst becoming an academy had improved their practice and their school, this was primarily because of the advantages generated by the collaborative framework of a multi-academy trust' (UK Parliament, 2015).

The trust creates a unique type of collaborative framework – and can create the culture and conditions for pupils and education professionals to benefit from it.

A strong and resilient structure

The second part of Munby's powerful question relates to structural resilience. Resilience is the capacity to recover quickly from difficulties. In organisational resilience theory, it also means the ability of an organisation to shape itself to respond to long-term challenges.

In the Introduction to this book, I wrote about the challenges Covid-19 will present for long-term economic, health, social and educational outcomes. On top of these challenges come more recent perturbations – global economic uncertainty, shifting macro global trends, and the impacts of all of this on our children, families and communities.

I think it is difficult to argue against a contention that we need to build the resilience of the school system in England. We need to do this in at least four ways – and our best bet for doing this is the structure of a group of schools:

- **Structural resilience** through groups of schools working together in a single legal entity with strong, strategic and focused governance.
- **Educational resilience** through the deeper knowledge building, collaboration and stronger conditions for building a culture of improvement. Our ability to better build, contest and renew the bodies of knowledge associated with education and running schools will make education more resilient to unevidenced fads and fashions.
- **Financial resilience** through greater economies of scale – ability to withstand further perturbations, with reduced competing demands from other essential services.
- **Workforce resilience** through an explicit focus on improving working conditions; and stronger, shared cultures built on relational trust, with evidence-informed professional development and pathways across schools, bolstering the recruitment, development and retention of teachers, leaders and support staff.

It is the single governance structure that binds schools together in an enduring partnership with an obligation to work through challenges together, rather than to separate at times of difficulty.

Every child a powerful learner

The third part of Munby's powerful question is the importance of understanding that every child is a powerful learner. In chapter three, I wrote about the need to think hard about how we create school environments where *all* children flourish, ensuring both the optimal continuing development of their intellectual potential and their ability to live well as rounded human beings.

Children are supported and enabled to be powerful learners in all types of school structures – and I want to honour the work that all schools do in this regard. I am definitely not claiming here that it is only the structure of the trust that enables children to be powerful learners. However, I am claiming that there is emerging evidence that in schools where the quality of education is not good enough, where the conditions are not right for children to be powerful learners, the trust appears to be our best bet for improvement.

Analysis comparing annual cohorts of 'sponsored academies'[12] with similar local authority-maintained schools shows that, on average, sponsored schools improve more quickly. Before they joined a trust, they performed significantly less well than otherwise similar schools. However, after joining a trust, the majority of sponsored academies demonstrate improvement, and their performance matches or exceeds these comparator schools. More than seven out of ten sponsored schools that were found to be underperforming as a local authority-maintained school in their previous inspection were found to have a 'good' or 'outstanding' rating (Department for Education, 2022).

I have argued that the trust is a knowledge-building structure (Bauckham and Cruddas, 2021). Chapter two set out a powerful model for implementing improvement at scale across a group of schools, in which every school in the trust mobilises its improvement capacity on behalf of the group, because they feel part of a single, focused, organisation.

Professional growth and development

The fourth part of Munby's powerful question is about the importance of professional growth and development. I explored in chapter five how a growing body of literature places teacher professional development at the heart of efforts to improve the school system.

As Barker and Patten state:

Pupils who benefit from more effective teaching not only learn more, they live happier and healthier lives (Jackson et al., 2014; Slater et al., 2012; Chetty et al., 2013).[13] The effect is strongest among pupils from disadvantaged backgrounds (Sutton Trust, 2011).[14] In order to improve the quality of teaching, we could try to recruit better teachers into the profession, but this is a slow and uncertain route, in part because it's hard to identify a great

---

12 A sponsored academy is a previously underperforming maintained school in need of support and/or judged 'inadequate' by Ofsted, where the law requires them to become academies.

13 See, for example, Jackson, Rockoff and Staiger (2014); Slater, Davies and Burgess (2012); Chetty, Friedman and Rockoff (2013).

14 See Sutton Trust (2011).

teacher right at the start of their career (Wiliam, 2016).[15] A better, and indeed a more ethical approach, is to focus our efforts on helping existing teachers to improve.

Barker and Patten (2022)

I am not talking here of the kind of legacy professional development that may have existed in 'Baker days' or in service training (so-called INSET) days. I am talking about the hard task of creating cultures and communities of improvement across professionals in a group of schools designed using the 'active ingredients' of professional development (Sims *et al.*, 2021). This is hard to do and not yet the norm in our education system, but I believe that the trust structure is uniquely well placed to do this.

As I argued in chapter five, citing Barker and Patten (2022), this is because school trusts can work to overcome some of the challenges associated with the design and implementation of high-quality professional development through leveraging their capacity (scale and expertise) alongside their ability to control systematically the conditions and culture in which all staff work and professional development takes place.

In a compelling series of blogs, Steve Rollett reflects on how trusts can create the conditions for teachers to connect to one another and to professional knowledge in ways that were previously impossible for too many teachers (Rollett, 2022a, 2022b).

The future of the school system resides in building on the best of what has gone before. Rollett attempts to describe some of the best practice that existed in some local authorities, and explains how these nascent professional connections can be more consistently and robustly built on, deepened and scaled up by trusts in the coming years.

This is a vision of trusts in which professional connections are not left to chance, or undermined by competing priorities, but rather hardwired into our schools.

Solidarity and interconnectedness

I will go further than Steve Munby's words now, because I want to explore two concepts that go to the heart of the question of 'Why a trust-led system?'

It is our solidarity and our interconnectedness – our shared sense of purpose and our execution of a shared mission – that will make a difference to

---

15   See Wiliam, D. (2016), Chapter 2.

the children and communities we serve. It is through this that we mobilise education as a force for social justice and wider common good.

A quick word here on autonomy. There is evidence that professional 'autonomy' is strongly associated with improved job satisfaction and a greater intention to stay in teaching (for example, Worth and Van den Brande, 2020). It may be more helpful to replace the word 'autonomy' in this context with teacher agency. Surely we are not arguing for a system in which teachers have complete independence from professional practice and can practise teaching free of the influence of research and evidence? No profession would embrace that definition of 'autonomy'. By virtue of being a professional we have a duty to remain connected to the knowledge and evidence of our profession. However, if we reframe this as professional agency, it is a much more compelling concept. Professional agency is a powerful motivator. It is this sense of agency that is achieved most powerfully through strong cultures of professional growth and development.

As professionals we should share a sense of obligation and accountability for the education of the nation's children. And it is the inherently collaborative structure of a school trust, that can make it more possible for teachers and leaders to put their expertise to best use at multiple schools to help improve the quality of education where their colleagues may be struggling.

Research in 2017 by the National Foundation for Educational Research found that

around one per cent of teaching staff who work in a school that is part of a trust, move to another school within the same trust each year. The largest trusts have more teachers and senior leaders moving to other schools within the same trust, particularly in trusts with schools that are geographically clustered closely together. Senior leaders are also more likely to move within trusts than classroom teachers. This staff movement within trusts also tends to be towards higher-FSM [free school meals] schools, whereas in general teachers tend to move away from such schools.

Worth (2017)

The research report recommended that as the legal employers of all staff in their schools, trusts have more flexibility to offer teachers and senior leaders the opportunity to work where they are most needed.[16]

This shows how the trust can be a protective structure, nurturing talent and building resilience through the shared endeavour of teaching and leading. This movement of talent towards schools with more disadvantaged pupils is potentially very important. It means that leaders who are committed to making a difference in schools in the most disadvantaged communities are supported to succeed through being part of a strong structure that can deploy resources and remain connected to a community of practice.

It is our sense of solidarity and interconnectedness in the pursuit of social justice that is our most powerful weapon for education that can change the world.

---

16   There is more to do. Worth, Hillary and DeLazzari's 'Teacher retention and turnover research interim report' (2017) showed a more complex picture of retention but conceded that one possible explanation of slightly higher rates of teachers leaving the profession in trusts is that staff movements from a school-based role to a role in a central team are not captured by the School Workforce Census, as only school-level data are collected, and would therefore count as leaving the profession. We need different approaches to the census that recognise the school trust as the legal entity.

References

Barker, J. and Patten, K. (2022). *Professional development in school trusts: capacity, conditions and culture*. CST. Available at: https://cstuk.org.uk/knowledge/guidance-and-policy/development-in-school-trusts-capacity-conditions-and-culture/.

Bauckham, I. and Cruddas, L. (2021). Knowledge building: school improvement at scale. CST. Available at: https://cstuk.org.uk/assets/pdfs/CST_Knowledge_Building_Whitepaper.pdf.

Chetty, R., Friedman, J.N. and Rockoff, J.E. (2013). *Measuring the Impacts of Teachers II: teacher value-added and student outcomes in adulthood*. NFER Working Paper 19424.

Cruddas, L. (2023). *Starting with why: why join a trust – and why a trust-based system?* CST. Available at: https://cstuk.org.uk/knowledge/guidance-and-policy/starting-with-why-why-join-a-trust-and-why-a-trust-based-system/.

Department for Education (2022). *The case for a fully trust-led system*. HM Government. Available at: https://assets.publishing.service.gov.uk/media/62865295d3bf7f1f433ae170/The_case_for_a_fully_trust-led_system.pdf.

Fullan, M. and Quinn, J. (2015). *Coherence: The Right Drivers in Action for Schools, Districts, and Systems*. Corwin.

Hargreaves, D.H. (2012). *A self-improving school system: towards maturity*. National College for School Leadership. Available at: https://assets.publishing.service.gov.uk/government/uploads/system/uploads/attachment_data/file/325908/a-self-improving-school-system-towards-maturity.pdf.

Jackson, K., Rockoff, J. and Staiger, D. (2014). 'Teacher effects and teacher-related policies', *Annual Review of Economics*, 6(1), 801–825.

Munby, S. (2019). *Imperfect Leadership*. Crown House Publishing.

Rollett, S. (2022a). *Hard wiring connections: Part 1 – Knowing*. Available at: https://cstuk.org.uk/news-publications/cst-blogs/hard-wiring-connections/.

Rollett, S. (2022b). *Hard wiring connections: Part 2 – Connecting*. Available at: https://cstuk.org.uk/news-publications/cst-blogs/hard-wiring-connections-part-2/.

Sims, S., Fletcher-Wood, H., O'Mara-Eves, A., Cottingham, S., Stansfield, C., Van Herwegen, J. and Anders, J. (2021). *What are the characteristics of effective teacher professional development? A systematic review &*

meta-analysis. Education Endowment Foundation. Available at: https://educationendowmentfoundation.org.uk/education-evidence/evidence-reviews/teacher-professional-development-characteristics.

Sinek, S. (2009). *Start with Why: How Great Leaders Inspire Everyone to Take Action*. Penguin.

Slater, H., Davies, N. and Burgess, S. (2012) 'Do teachers matter? Measuring the variation in teacher effectiveness in England', *Oxford Bulletin of Economics and Statistics*, 74(5), 629–645.

Sutton Trust, The (2011). *Improving the impact of teachers on pupil achievement in the UK: interim findings*. The Sutton Trust. Available at: https://www.suttontrust.com/wp-content/uploads/2020/01/2teachers-impact-report-final.pdf.

UK Parliament (2015). *Education – fourth report: academies and free schools*. House of Commons Education Committee. Available at: https://publications.parliament.uk/pa/cm201415/cmselect/cmeduc/258/25802.htm.

Wiliam, D. (2016). *Leadership for Teacher Learning: Creating a Culture Where All Teachers Improve So That All Students Succeed*. Learning Sciences International.

Worth, J. (2017). *Teacher retention and turnover research – research update 2: teacher dynamics in multi-academy trusts*. NFER. Available at: https://www.nfer.ac.uk/publications/teacher-retention-and-turnover-research-research-update-2-teacher-dynamics-in-multi-academy-trusts/.

Worth, J. and Van den Brande, J. (2020). *Teacher autonomy: how does it relate to job satisfaction and retention?* National Foundation for Educational Research and Teacher Development Trust. Available at: https://www.nfer.ac.uk/publications/teacher-autonomy-how-does-it-relate-to-job-satisfaction-and-retention/.

Worth, J., Hillary, J. and DeLazzari, G. (2017). *Teacher retention and turnover research: interim report*. Available at: https://www.nfer.ac.uk/publications/teacher-retention-and-turnover-research-interim-report/.

CHAPTER TWELVE
SYSTEM BUILDING: ACTING *ON*, RATHER THAN JUST ACTING *IN* THE SYSTEM

Whereas the previous chapter argued that, as system builders, we need to make the strong evidence-informed and purpose-driven case as to why a group of schools working together in deep and purposeful collaboration in a single legal entity is our best bet, this chapter asks leaders to go even further. It invites you to 'see' the system. The Government Office for Science defines a system as 'a set of elements or parts interconnected in such a way that they may produce their own, potentially unexpected, pattern of behaviour over time' (Government Office for Science, 2023). I would suggest that this definition is actually the definition of a complex adaptive system.

In chapter seven, I briefly outlined some of the features of complex adaptive systems. I wrote about how small directed actions can cause large changes in aggregate behaviour through lever points. I wrote about self-organisation and emergence: 'Complex systems self-organise, i.e. autonomously change their behaviour or modify their structure, to eliminate or reduce the impact of disruptive events (adaptability) or to repel attacks (resilience)' (Rzevski and Skobelev, 2014, p. 9).

The reason that complexity theory is important to me is that it highlights the power of agents (leaders), and agency. I concluded the Introduction to this book with these words: we need leaders who have the expertise, the professional will and professional generosity to contribute to system improvement as a form of system building. In this way, we will leverage leadership of the school system and enable the vastly more powerful and sustainable school system to be born.

This chapter explores four such system interventions – where leaders have come together to act *on*, rather than just *in*, local, regional and national systems. In all of these examples, the system leaders have mobilised forms of collective leadership. They have not attempted to make the system intervention on their own. These case studies are characterised by professional generosity and reciprocity.

To use the language of the King's Fund report on the practice of system leadership, they start with a coalition of the willing, build an evidence base and build outwards; they demonstrate constancy of purpose combined with a degree of flexibility, and stability of leadership (Timmins, 2015).

They are the collective work of leaders acting on the system to create the conditions for wider system improvement.

They are examples of the deliberate act of system building.

Acting on a local system: the Plymouth example

Plymouth's school improvement initiative

Plymouth, Britain's Atlantic city, with a population of approximately 270,000, has operated as a unitary authority since 1998.

The challenge and problem that place-based working aims to solve is the significant and stubbornly persistent underperformance of students at key stage 4 across the city as a whole. Despite the efforts and expertise of many dedicated professionals, Plymouth has consistently ranked below the national average in terms of GCSE attainment and progress. This has serious implications for the life chances, wellbeing and aspirations of young people in Plymouth, as well as the economic and social development of the city.

Historically, there have been various attempts to foster collaboration and coordination among schools and other educational stakeholders in Plymouth, such as headteacher phase associations, local authority networks and services, outreach initiatives, teaching school alliances and other professional networks. However, none of these initiatives has been able to achieve a sustained and systemic impact on the quality of teaching and learning and the outcomes of students. The collaboration that existed was often superficial, fragmented, and driven by external agendas rather than by a shared vision and commitment to improvement.

The recognition and agreement across stakeholders that GCSE outcomes presented as the 'burning platform' for change was the catalyst for place-based working. There was a collective sense of urgency and responsibility to address the situation and to explore new ways of working that would be more effective, inclusive and sustainable. Place-based working emerged as a promising approach that would leverage the strengths, resources and potential of the local context, while also drawing on external expertise and capacity.

The collective actors included school leaders, further education leaders, local authority leaders and the DfE through the regional director. Local trusts involved in the Plymouth initiative include Westcountry Schools Trust, Ted Wragg Trust, Reach South Academy Trust and Plymouth CAST. Greenshaw Learning Trust and the Thinking Schools Trust also provided capacity and expertise, and many colleagues mention their system generosity. Transforming Futures Trust provided expertise in special education. The approach is supported by a range of strategic and operational partners, such as the local teaching school hub and the Education Endowment Foundation.

The Plymouth place-based approach recognises the diversity and autonomy of these actors but also seeks to create a culture of collaboration and trust among them, by fostering a sense of belonging, identity and ownership of the city and its children. The Plymouth place-based approach also aims to establish a clear and coherent strategic vision and plan for the city, based on a robust and shared understanding of the needs, strengths and aspirations of the children and young people. The Plymouth place-based approach is not only a vision and a plan, but also a process and a practice of mobilising the collective capacity and collaboration of all the actors in the city to improve the outcomes for all children.

The 'bind' between actors strengthened as each was allocated oversight and lead of a strand of the collective improvement plan. The system generosity of the external expertise introduced to the city came to the fore for the good of all. Strands of the plan included school leadership development, curriculum development, key stage 2 to key stage 3 transition (the transition from primary to secondary school), reducing pupil mobility and developing pedagogy.

Governance of the place-based approach was key to ensuring continued collaboration and successful delivery of the plan. The model of leadership, governance and accountability is based on the concept of 'networked governance', which involves multiple and distributed forms of leadership and decision-making, and shared and mutual forms of accountability. The governance of the work is now in its third iteration, but at all times the governance group has been chaired by a trust leader. The chair of the governance group has been a member of, and reported to, the Plymouth Education Board.

As governance and school improvement activity matured, 'professional trust' strengthened, which enabled more of an 'open book' approach to sharing, and real-time, transparent data sharing became easier.

The impact of the place-based approach is already evident. Plymouth's secondary schools are less vulnerable, with improved inspection outcomes and GCSE results. In 2023, higher Attainment 8 and Progress 8 scores were achieved, and the number of pupils securing good passes in English and maths increased. Further improvements are anticipated for summer 2024.

The place-based work is believed to be sustainable since the approach is driven by the 'sector', and the 'bind' of actors together is secure. Plans and strategies will no doubt evolve, but they will do so for all the children of Plymouth.

Acting on a regional system: the Education Exchange and Reconnect London

The Education Exchange

The Education Exchange[17] is a group of strategic partners in the north of England, based around Yorkshire, who exist to drive achievement, address disadvantage, and raise the aspirations of the children and communities they serve. It aims to unite educators in sustainable professional friendships, ensuring all children can enjoy success irrespective of their starting points.

The Education Exchange is an alliance of trusts and trust leaders. There are no financial costs or payments involved. The alliance is simply a commitment from friends that if they take something from the exchange, they are prepared to offer something themselves if asked.

The Education Exchange aims to:

- improve inclusion by transforming outcomes, especially for disadvantaged pupils and pupils with SEND
- place collaboration before competition, working openly with those who are keen to offer support and those who are keen to receive it

---

17   More information about the Education Exchange can be found online: https://educationexchange.org.uk.

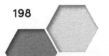

- contribute expertise and mobilise resources to improve education together
- focus on what works in schools, and what is proven to be effective
- show respect for context, as different schools often face different challenges
- give, accept and reflect on feedback to drive continuous improvement
- recognise that economic future prosperity is inextricably linked to the quality of education.

Support for schools: intensive transition engagement to support rapid improvement

The Education Exchange has offered intensive transition engagement to two schools: Brooksbank School and Milton Special School. Both were placed in special measures, with significant safeguarding concerns. In both cases, the regional director at the DfE approached the Education Exchange to lead projects to provide school improvement support.

Within a short time frame, a team of education professionals with significant experience in rapid school improvement were brought together to support each school. Working as part of the Education Exchange partnership, a large number of experienced senior leaders came together and swiftly implemented structural and systematic changes to ensure the safeguarding of pupils and to support high standards in each school.

Support for trusts

The Education Exchange team worked intensively with the primary team at the White Horse Federation, providing professional development, tracking and intervention systems. The proportion of children meeting the expected standards in reading, writing and maths rose by 5% across the whole trust in the 2023–24 academic year. The collaboration has raised standards and forged new friendships.

Launchpad for Literacy

The Education Exchange has also worked alongside local authorities on specific initiatives. An example of this is the Launchpad for Literacy project, which launched in summer 2021 with Barnsley Local Authority.

The project is delivered alongside the Launchpad for Literacy creator. Launchpad for Literacy is a systematic, skill-based approach, improving outcomes in the early years and beyond by identifying and closing specific skills gaps. It ensures that practitioners have a greater level of diagnostic capability, establishing reasons and solutions to underpin informed interventions.

Schools applied, received the resources and were invited to an introductory session to demonstrate using the toolkit. A second cohort took place in spring 2022. A total of 73 schools have benefited from a programme of professional development and a series of face-to-face and virtual training sessions.

Quality assurance

The Education Exchange has worked alongside school and trust leaders to establish rigorous and reliable quality assurance systems. Introducing a coherent system of quality assurance allows for professional engagement with a wide range of stakeholders and external agencies, using a common language of school improvement. This system of quality assurance enables the alignment of self-evaluation with future planning and facilitates rapid improvement.

Delta Academies Trust and New Collaborative: a virtuous circle

Delta Academies Trust is one of the lead partners in the Education Exchange, and gives generously of its expertise and resources. When New Collaborative, a very high-performing post-16 group, took on the sponsorship of a number of secondary schools, it reached out to the Education Exchange for help. The Delta team provided support on curriculum and staffing structures. The payback for this generosity was huge. Delta successfully bid for a post-16 free school. Following a call from Delta, New Collaborative provided curriculum plans, staffing plans, school day structures and even building plans. These were with the Delta team within 24 hours, saving months of work and many thousands of pounds for the taxpayer. You cannot underestimate the power of having friends.

The future

The concept of the Education Exchange is generating interest in other regions. There are now plans for trust leaders to establish a group to create an Education Exchange in the north-east. Another group of trust leaders is planning to establish an Education Exchange in Birmingham. There is also a new project team with similar ambitions in the Liverpool region.

Reconnect London

Reconnect London[18] exists to help schools to bring about positive change in the lives of young Londoners.

In 2020, during the Covid-19 pandemic, a group of headteachers and trust leaders came together to form Reconnect London. The aim was to support headteachers with the many immediate issues they were facing at that time, by drawing on the collective expertise of the group.

A key initial focus was to use their expertise to help other schools to improve the attendance and engagement of children and young people during the pandemic. Since that time, Reconnect London has evolved to have a broader focus on the key challenges facing London schools, and the need for innovative approaches to meet these challenges.

It supports school leaders to find innovative solutions to collective challenges, through:

- a Knowledge Lab, which produces research that contributes to better understanding of the challenges facing London schools
- an Innovation Lab, which supports headteachers to work together on practical projects aimed at addressing specific issues or challenges in their schools
- a Headteacher Network through which knowledge, expertise and good practice are shared
- a leadership development programme, 'London Leaders', which promotes and facilitates place-based approaches to school improvement in the capital.

Reconnect London is committed to taking action collectively to improve the lives of young Londoners. Its approach is characterised by connectivity, collaboration and cooperation. The knowledge and expertise of experienced school, trust and local authority leaders, alongside third-sector and corporate partners, are mobilised to bring about positive change.

Reconnect London takes an assets-based approach, emphasising the strengths and resources that exist within communities that may be perceived as marginalised or minoritised, as well as the challenges

18   More information about Reconnect London can be found online: https://reconnectlondon.org.

they face. It does not attempt to speak for others, but seeks to create space for all local stakeholders, including children and young people, to participate in discussions and decision-making processes.

A key focus for Reconnect London has been the development and implementation of a practitioner-led model for the sourcing of school-to-school support. Working closely with the regional director and her team at the DfE, Reconnect London has created and implemented an approach that centres around a School-to-School Support Steering Group, comprising 10 experienced system leaders. The group receives requests for help from schools and trusts that are experiencing significant challenges, and deploys intensive leadership support for them. Very positive feedback has been received about the impact of the support provided. Reconnect London is launching Leaders for London, which intends to train the next generation of leaders to be able to undertake this kind of intensive school-to-school support work. It is working with a range of partners – both within London and beyond.

Reconnect London is working with ImpactEd to develop an evaluation framework that will enable it to robustly assess the impact of its work.

Acting on a national system: the School-Led Development Trust and the National Institute of Teaching

In January 2021, the then Secretary of State announced plans for a new National Institute of Teaching, intended to provide teachers and school leaders with prestigious training and development. The intention was for this national initiative to deliver evidence-based approaches to teacher training, and also include mentoring and early career support, alongside leadership courses and continued professional development. The then government announced a national procurement and said that the institute would be funded as part of the £22 million for teacher quality agreed at the 2020 Spending Review.

A group of four trusts that were already working closely together during the pandemic – the Harris Federation, Oasis Community Learning, Outwood Grange Academies Trust and Star Academies – established a charity called the School-Led Development Trust (SLDT). Its charitable objects are the product of the four trusts' foundational beliefs: to advance education, learning and research for the public benefit, including through investigating, trialling and delivering educator development so all English schools benefit. The SLDT was subsequently awarded the contract to run the National Institute of Teaching. This is its story:

The National Institute of Teaching

By Melanie Renowden, founding chief executive of the National Institute of Teaching

Perhaps unexpectedly, it was the unique circumstances confronting school leaders in 2020 at the start of the Covid-19 pandemic which helped to set the conditions that led to the creation of the National Institute of Teaching.

As the school sector battled to respond to the unprecedented demands of Covid-19, contact, cooperation and innovation among trust leaders increased substantially. Faced with unknowns such as mass virtual education and social distancing, trusts quickly recognised that they could serve their children and communities more effectively if they pooled knowledge, resources and learning. And this rapid collaboration generated three important enablers of the partnership from which the National Institute grew: opportunity, arising from the increased contact time during the Covid-19 period; proof-points, with successful collaborations created during the pandemic building confidence in the value of partnership working; and trust, with relationships built and deepened by the exceptionally demanding experience of leading a public service during the pandemic.

And so, in the margins of discussions about emergency response, another conversation started. One that coalesced around a unifying factor: the critical importance of – but continued difficulty with – retaining, developing and recruiting staff.

Schools, and indeed trusts, have long recognised their responsibility to develop their teaching staff in pursuit of educational excellence. Indeed, many trusts – including those behind the National Institute – go beyond this, collaborating with others to grow and retain teaching staff.

But, despite this, quality teaching is not evenly distributed across the English school system, we don't know enough about the best ways to develop it, and it is hampered by persistent challenges with teacher retention and recruitment. In practice, this means that the children whose lives can be most positively affected by great teaching too often miss out.

It was this reality that prompted those first four trusts to take their conversations one bold step further and establish the School-Led Development Trust, which subsequently became the National Institute of Teaching.

With their large networks of schools, wide geographic footprints, varied settings and long-standing commitment to communities facing socio-economic disadvantage, the four trusts share many structural similarities. They also are united by a core set of beliefs, on which the National Institute is founded:

- that effective teacher and leader preparation and development can increase teacher wellbeing, retention, recruitment and quality
- that research evidence can help understand the most effective teacher and leader preparation and development practices
- that bringing research and front-line practice together will increase the positive impact of teacher development interventions on children's outcomes.

The creation of the National Institute represented a next evolutionary step for the trusts, and built on an extensive heritage. The four trusts had long acted on their belief in the power of quality teaching, both individually and in partnerships. They had run initial teacher training, they had opened their own staff training centres, they had even come together with other partners to create a forerunner to the National Institute to offer national professional qualifications (NPQs).

But the ambition to deliver benefit well beyond the boundaries of their own trusts has required a different approach. In service of the system-wide mission of the National Institute, each of the four founder trusts has had to dismantle, to relinquish and to cede control – in other words, to look beyond the short-term needs of their own organisations in pursuit of long-term benefit for all children in the school system.

Manifestations of this commitment include the closure of the successful school-centred initial teacher training at Star Academies and the Harris Federation, the winding up of the School-Led Network national professional qualifications provider, the trusts' hosting of the National Institute's physical campuses, and the transfer of valued staff. Crucially, it is also baked in to the governance of the School-Led Development Trust, with the deliberate decision to ensure a majority of trustees are independent of the founding trust partnership. It's these tangible, and sometimes difficult, enactments of the guiding principles behind the National Institute that help to set us up for success, and that push us from the 'softer' aligned cooperation to the necessarily 'harder' collaborative partnership.

The CEOs of the four founding trusts, now joined in the National Institute community by our Associate College trust partners, have taken these decisions because they recognise that to act meaningfully on the system requires the delicate balancing of organisational and national interests. They know that holding the course towards tangible system-level impact will require long-term persistence. And they understand that their chances of success are increased when they act deliberately in concert with one another.

It's still early days for the National Institute of Teaching. Our inaugural national cohort of 500 trainees have just finished their training and secured jobs in schools across the country, our first research insights have been published and our work with the CEOs of school trusts is underway. We're realistic about the challenges ahead, and we know that we will need to pull hard against the normal forces of organisation evolution as they act to drag us away from our school roots. But we're also ambitious with our plans to overcome these hurdles and believe that the trust-led foundations we've established give us the very best possible chance of success. On behalf of all of our children.

System leadership as a collective act

In chapter eight, I explored Senge, Hamilton and Kania's three core capabilities to foster collective leadership. I am going to return to these core capabilities here to demonstrate how the ability to act on a system often requires collective acts of leadership (Senge, Hamilton and Kania, 2015).

The ability to see the larger system

In all four case studies in this chapter, the leaders who worked together demonstrated their ability to see the larger system. They developed a shared understanding of the issue they were seeking to address and then worked collaboratively to develop solutions that were probably not evident to any of them individually but also were likely to be beyond the capacity of individuals or single institutions. They acted together for the health of the whole system – local, regional or national.

Fostering reflection and generative conversations

Senge, Hamilton and Kania define reflection as 'thinking about our thinking', or holding up the mirror to see the taken-for-granted assumptions. In each of the case studies above, the leaders did not allow their own mental models to limit the work. Instead they developed a deep and shared understanding. They constructed a shared reality. This is essential for fostering collective creativity.

Shifting the collective focus from reactive problem-solving to co-creating the future

Senge, Hamilton and Kania reflect that change often starts with conditions that are undesirable. This is certainly true of the Plymouth example. What this example shows is how skilful leaders help people move beyond just reacting to these problems to building positive visions for the future.

In the Plymouth example, this happened gradually as leaders worked together to articulate their deeper aspirations and built confidence based on tangible accomplishments achieved together. As Senge, Hamilton and Kania propose, this shift involves not just building inspiring visions but facing difficult truths about the present reality, and learning how to use the tension between vision and reality to inspire truly new approaches.

References

Government Office for Science (2023). *The civil servant's system thinking journey*. HM Government. Available at: https://www.gov.uk/government/publications/systems-thinking-for-civil-servants/journey.

Rzevski, G. and Skobelev, P. (2014). *Managing Complexity*. WIT Press.

Senge, P., Hamilton, H. and Kania, J. (2015). 'The dawn of system leadership', *Stanford Social Innovation Review*, Winter. Available at: https://ssir.org/articles/entry/the_dawn_of_system_leadership#.

Timmins, N. (2015). *The practice of system leadership: being comfortable with chaos*. The King's Fund. Available at: https://assets.kingsfund.org.uk/f/256914/x/ada1cf3947/practice_system_leadership_2015.pdf.

CHAPTER THIRTEEN
CURATING THE PIPELINE OF THE NEXT GENERATION OF LEADERS

One of the important aspects of system building is building the pipeline of the next generation of leaders. This is a system leadership challenge because the school system in England can only take the next step if we have identified, supported and developed the next generation of school and trust leaders.

There are several potential problems that we need to face as the system of school trusts in England grows, and our knowledge, theories and practices evolve.

The first is that that we need a model of trust leadership that goes beyond competency-based or generic models of leadership typically focused only on organisational leadership. Competency is the application of the specific knowledge, skills and attitudes that are needed to undertake a work role. As Leesa Wheelahan (2010) has pointed out, the problem with any competency-based training is that it ties knowledge and skill directly to workplace performances and roles, and not to systematic structured disciplinary systems of meaning.

If our focus remains just on *organisational* leadership, we run the risk that the school trust becomes another insular, inward-looking structure with little connection to its civic context and little interest in the wider system. This is potentially dangerous because it could feed self-interest, acquisitive growth that is harmful to the local education economy, a focus on 'outcomes' for the children in 'my' organisation at the expense of others, and a belligerent system divided up into competitive fiefdoms.

Leadership narratives and programmes that keep us tied only to organisational competencies and leadership genericism will not produce the leaders or the system of schooling we need in England.

This requires that we not merely shift our mental models of leadership but forge a new mental model. We need a radically different approach to leadership development that is not based on the tired rehearsal of leadership competencies or genericism, but rather gives access to higher-order knowledge and thinking.

We need to develop systems of meaning that provide more access to theoretical knowledge than the weakly classified knowledge of competency-based programmes, with their focus only on the field of practice.

We need to build secure mental models based on a body of knowledge, so that trust leaders are not just able to contribute to society's conversations about schooling, but to actively shape them. At CST, it is my hope that we have begun the task of classifying the knowledge required to lead school trusts as a field of study.

Leadership genericism and domain-specific knowledge

A heated debate has existed for the last few years about whether leadership is a generic set of skills or domain-specific knowledge. This matters because our leadership development programmes are underpinned by a theory of knowledge.

In a brilliant exposition of this in two blogs, Tom Rees and Jen Barker (formerly of Ambition Institute) propose that this dichotomy is unhelpful, but it is also not quite right to say that the answer is both leadership genericism and domain-specific knowledge. They write:

Whilst it might intuitively sound right that leadership development should focus on both generic and domain-specific approaches, this view is built on the assumption that generic and domain-specific bodies of knowledge are two different things. We think such a view misses the important connection between them, specifically that a generic skill, when broken down into component parts, consists largely of knowledge from within a given domain, be that formal knowledge or knowledge of the context and people we work with.

Barker and Rees (2021)

They conclude that educational leadership requires knowledge from other fields – this is true of school leadership and even more the case for trust leadership. They also believe that generic skills rely specifically on knowledge – however, knowledge does not transfer easily across domains.

They are persuaded that rather than organising a curriculum for leadership development around a set of generic leadership capabilities, a better starting point is to organise leadership development around the core responsibilities of school leaders' roles. This is where we started in beginning to codify the knowledge required to lead a trust.

Beginning the task of codifying the knowledge required to lead a trust

In July 2022, the then Minister for the School and College System, Baroness Barran, established an advisory group to develop a content framework for trust leadership development. I was pleased to be invited to serve on this advisory group. This was the first real attempt to codify a body of knowledge that would inform development programmes for those leading school trusts.

The framework (Department for Education, 2023) attempted to codify the knowledge, skills and behaviours across six domains for strong trust leadership:

1. **Leadership and Organisational Development**, setting out how a CEO can create a cohesive organisational culture focused on providing a structure through which staff and pupils can thrive.

2. **Quality of Education**, explaining the fundamental role a CEO has in providing the strongest possible education for children in their schools.

3. **Strategic Governance**, showing how the best CEOs work within robust governance structures and are ably supported by their boards.

4. **Finance and Operations**, providing an overview of the financial management and operational systems CEOs need to employ to ensure the sustainability of the education they deliver and the growth of the trust.

5. **Workforce and Talent Development**, underpinning the ways in which CEOs interact with their staff, offering opportunities for professional development across their trusts.

6. **Public Benefit and Civic Duty**, detailing the role CEOs play in prioritising the legal and moral imperative of trusts as education charities.

CST's thought leadership contributed significantly to this work. The framework aligns extremely closely with both the publication of 'Building strong trusts' (Cruddas, 2023) and 'The core responsibilities of a school trust chief executive officer' (CST, 2021), which are the CEO standards that CST developed with our community in 2021.

The framework acknowledges: 'We have used the best available evidence to construct the content framework, though we acknowledge the limited quantitative evidence that exists at the leadership level in relation to the running of large trusts. The evidence base has been gathered by integrating expertise with empirical research' (Department for Education, 2023, p. 8).

The framework begins the task of classifying the knowledge required to lead school trusts as a field of study, but it is nowhere near a settled or satisfactory state. It is more a collection of resources than a body of knowledge. There is so much more we need to understand about this field of practice in order to curate the body of knowledge. We must lead this work together and build the evidence base about leadership knowledge and practice.

Building the pipeline of the next generation of leaders

Curating the body of knowledge is one task in building the pipeline of leaders. If we are to build a schooling system in England where every school is part of a strong trust, we need to develop a strategy to secure the pipeline of trust leaders. I believe that this requires a talent management strategy and that it should be sector led.

As the sector and employer body, CST will hold this strategy, while we simultaneously curate the body of knowledge. We are developing the strategy in seven parts:

1. Workforce analytics
2. People and organisational standards
3. Building the talent pool
4. Next-generation CEO development
5. Increasing diversity
6. Talent acquisition, including recruitment
7. Support in role.

As the holder of strategy, we want the sector to step forward in system leadership roles to develop the next generation of leadership programmes.

I want to explore just one system intervention – where leaders have come together, once again, to act *on*, rather than just *in* their regional system. These system leaders have established collective leadership in an attempt to secure a pipeline of leaders in the south-west. This initiative is scalable and is now being rolled out to other regions in England.

Curating the pipeline of the next generation of leaders
SW100

Headteachers are perhaps the most important people in our education system. They have a profound influence on the extent to which children and staff at their school are able to thrive. Yet in many parts of the country, recruiting headteachers is a challenge, especially in schools serving under-resourced communities.

This was the case in Devon and Cornwall in 2020. Multiple trust leaders were wrestling with the challenge; all were trying lots of ways to attract great people to their schools, but the approaches felt overly reliant on lucky timing with a few good people. A more systemic approach to developing the leadership pipeline was needed. In an excellent example of system leadership, a group of trust leaders came together to develop one.

The Ted Wragg Trust, Education South West and Westcountry Schools Trust came together with the Reach Foundation to create SW100, a one-year programme for aspiring headteachers in Devon and Cornwall. They were soon joined by Dartmoor Multi Academy Trust, Cornwall Education Learning Trust, Learning Academies Trust, Kernow Learning, and Truro and Penwith Academy Trust.

Over five years, SW100 aims to identify and develop 100 future headteachers in Devon and Cornwall with a shared commitment to eradicating educational inequity. Several principles underpin the programme:

1. Made (together) in the South West

SW100 was co-created by the partner trust leaders. As a result, there is a genuine shared ownership of the programme. Co-creating and running SW100 *together* has ensured a shared focus on building a strong leadership pipeline for *all* schools. It is made in the South West for leaders in the South West, and there is a shared purpose that transcends any individual trust: enabling *all* children in the South West to enjoy lives of choice and opportunity.

2. Locally rooted ...

SW100 starts with understanding the local context. Asking 'How can we develop headteachers to run great schools *in Devon and Cornwall?*' demands a more nuanced answer than asking 'How can we develop headteachers to run great schools?'

Building a deeper understanding of their communities enables participants to develop *specific* solutions to challenges, drawing on local assets and contextual knowledge as well as nationally available evidence. The local focus pushes participants to understand how to make effective *use* of evidence in their schools. By making this a collective endeavour, we reduce the burden on individual leaders to translate evidence into their own context. Through understanding our communities more deeply, our commitment to them is strengthened.

3. ... and nationally connected
The SW100 focus on understanding local context is combined with a commitment to helping all participants feel 'nationally connected'. Through visits to multiple schools and trusts across the country, participants gain new perspectives on their own struggles and successes, and learn from school leaders who are pushing the boundaries in supporting children experiencing disadvantage. These visits are about stimulus, not solutions. Long bus rides home provide opportunities for long discussions and deep reflection, and nurture an increased collective sense of possibility.

4. Relationships matter
SW100 invests heavily in relationships between leaders in a local area. Residential elements of the programme are held in self-catered houses where participants cook together, learn together and build the trust required to challenge one another's thinking. Mirroring the co-creation of the programme by trust leaders, these relationships galvanise school leaders around the shared purpose of challenging disadvantage in *their* region. Several SW100 alumni who are now headteachers have said they would not have applied for their roles without the support of peers in their cohort. A collective will to lead change locally is developed and legitimised, and participants develop a *shared* courage to act.

5. Clarity of purpose
Finally, SW100 is designed to help participants clarify what really matters to them as a leader *before* they step into headship. In a rapidly changing system, clarity of purpose is more important than ever. Schools are the 'last institutions' in many communities and – as a result – leaders are under pressure both within and beyond the school gates. This presents a significant opportunity for schools and trusts to reimagine their roles within their communities. But to influence widely and partner successfully so all children can thrive, leaders need a clear

direction and the agility to navigate untrodden paths. This is what the SW100 programme aims to help leaders do.

The SW100 programme is showing significant promise. The third cohort have just completed the programme and already (despite the programme being aimed at people wishing to become headteachers within five years) close to 40% of alumni from cohorts 1–3 have already secured headteacher roles.

This success has inspired the co-creation of similar programmes by trust leaders in the West Country (West100), Yorkshire (Yorks100) and the East of England (East100). It has also inspired the co-creation – by partner trust CEOs – of LeadingTrusts, which is based on similar principles to SW100.

LeadingTrusts

The current generation of school trust leaders established the trust sector. Together, they have shown that trusts can lead significant improvement in our schools – especially for children experiencing disadvantage. But the challenges and opportunities awaiting the next generation of trust CEOs continue to evolve rapidly in scale and scope.

Recognising this, SW100, West100 and Yorks100 partner trusts worked together with the Reach Foundation to develop LeadingTrusts, a leadership programme that aims to develop a new generation of trust CEOs to lead the next iteration of school trusts.

For many future leaders, the role of trust CEO remains a bit of a mystery. Opportunities to properly understand both the job at hand and the massive opportunities it provides to lead transformational change for our children are few and far between. LeadingTrusts creates the time and space for leaders to developing a deep understanding of the trust CEO role; sharpen their thinking about the kind of CEO they would like to be; and builds a strong network of future CEOs (both within their regions and beyond) to work towards a shared ambition of a future where *every* child thrives in our schools.

LeadingTrusts is possible because of the extraordinary system generosity of current trust CEOs. Each year, at least a dozen leaders take time to share their wisdom with the new generation of leaders. In the inaugural year of the programme, the cohort met with Dame Alice Hudson (Twyford Church of England Academies Trust), Sir Jon Coles (United Learning), Aidan Sadgrove (Brigshaw Learning Partnership), Luke Sparkes (Dixons Academies), Sir Mufti Hamid Patel CBE (Star Academies), Gail Brown

(Ebor Academy Trust), Dr Vanessa Ogden CBE (Mulberry Schools Trust), Jonny Uttley (The Education Alliance), Nick Osborne (Maritime Academy Trust) and Sir Dan Moynihan (Harris Federation). They also meet with leaders from Apple, Deloitte and the Boston Consulting Group.

Through detailed discussions with such a range of leaders, LeadingTrusts participants deepen their understanding of how current trust CEOs achieved their success, and spark ideas about future breakthroughs for the sector.

Collectively, by 2029, these school and trust leadership programmes aim to develop a movement of 200 future trust CEOs and 400 future headteachers, all of whom are driven by a desire to enable *all* children to enjoy lives of choice and opportunity. And it all started with an act of collective system leadership in the South West

References

Barker, J. and Rees, T. (2021). *Beyond the generic/domain-specific leadership dichotomy*. Ambition Institute. Available at: https://www.ambition.org.uk/blog/beyond-genericdomain-specific-leadership-dichotomy/?s=09.

Cruddas, L. (2023). *Building strong trusts*. CST. Available at: https://cstuk.org.uk/knowledge/guidance-and-policy/building-strong-trusts/.

CST (2021). *The core responsibilities of a school trust chief executive officer*. Available at: https://cstuk.org.uk/assets/link_boxes/Guidances/CEO-Core-Responsibilities-November-2021.pdf.

Department for Education (2023). *Multi-academy trust leadership development: chief executive officer content framework*. HM Government. Available at: https://assets.publishing.service.gov.uk/media/64ff30a657278000142518db/MAT_leadership_development_-_CEO_content_framework.pdf.

Wheelahan, L. (2010). 'The structure of pedagogic discourse as a relay for power: the case of competency-based training, toolkits, translation devices and conceptual accounts', in Singh, P., Sadovnik, A. and Semel, S. (eds), *Toolkits, Translation Devices and Conceptual Accounts: Essays on Basil Bernstein's Sociology of Knowledge*, pp. 47–63. Peter Lang Publishing.

CHAPTER FOURTEEN
CREATING THE CONDITIONS FOR THE SYSTEM TO KEEP GETTING BETTER

I want to turn now to another aspect of system building – this is how we build:

- system resilience
- system improvement
- system architecture
- system governance.

Each of these is essential for the school system in England to keep getting better.

System resilience

In chapter eleven, I argued that our best bet for building system resilience is the structure of a group of schools working together in deep and purposeful collaboration:

- **Structural resilience** through groups of schools working together in a single legal entity with strong, strategic and focused governance.
- **Educational resilience** through the deeper knowledge building, collaboration and stronger conditions for building a culture of improvement. Our ability to better build, contest and renew the bodies of knowledge associated with education and running schools will make education more resilient to unevidenced fads and fashions.
- **Financial resilience** through greater economies of scale – ability to withstand further perturbations, with reduced competing demands from other essential services.
- **Workforce resilience** through an explicit focus on improving working conditions; and stronger, shared cultures built on relational trust, with evidence-informed professional development and pathways across schools, bolstering the recruitment, development and retention of teachers, leaders and support staff.

I argued that we need a powerful evidence-informed, purpose-driven narrative to make the case that all schools should be part of a group.

The word resilience originated from the Latin word *resiliere*, which means to 'bounce back'. Hosseini, Barker and Ramirez-Marquez use the following definition: 'The common use of resilience word implies the ability of an entity or system to return to normal condition after the occurrence of an event that disrupts its state' (Hosseini, Barker and Ramirez-Marquez, 2016).

Given the analysis in the Introduction to this book of the multiple negative impacts of the global pandemic, followed sharply by a global economic crisis, climate disasters, social unrest, global political instability, and conflicts and wars, all of which are likely to determine our future, it is essential that our schooling system is resilient and can withstand further perturbations.

I believe there is an important duty of government to rebuild the resilience of the state school system and wider public services in England. Only government can pull some of the big strategic levers that would enable this to happen. But I don't think we should rely solely on a state actor.

Trust leaders as system builders have a role too. We can make the case for groups of schools because evidence-informed improvement models and shared cultures of improvement are our best bet for a school system that keeps getting better. Over time, as more schools join trusts, this will also build system coherence. It will also build the strategic resilience of our school system.

But we must also act as civic leaders in the places in which our schools are located, to build local resilience. We can, as I explored in the second part of this book, build connected systems and forms of radical collaboration that find solutions to the problems our schools, children, families and communities face. These small directed actions will add up. We know from complex adaptive systems these generally follow a discernible pattern – in essence, a new order.

What we do now, what we do next, matters hugely. We are (or must become) the leaders we have been waiting for.

System improvement

The National Audit Office good practice guidance on principles of effective regulation says regulators should consider the 'range and effectiveness of existing powers in achieving regulatory objectives – including "softer" influencing powers as well as "hard" enforcement powers – and how to deal with different types of problem as well as new challenges' (National Audit Office, 2021).

Furthermore, it says regulators should hold a theory of change. The existing regulatory theory of change has been largely based on harder forms of intervention, typified by the ability of the regulator to sponsor a maintained school into a trust, or 're-broker' an academy school.

The school system has undergone a significant shift, with many schools having chosen to become an academy or been sponsored into trusts, including many of those that had previously been underperforming over a long period. There is evidence that school trusts have been particularly effective in improving education in these circumstances, and it is crucial the regulator maintains this lever moving forward (Ofsted, 2020; Department for Education, 2022).

Doing so is not an arbitrary expression of preferred structures or ideologies, as some claim; it is in fact a regulatory commitment to the principle of sound governance. Where we see significant failures in educational standards, it is right that governance arrangements can be changed by moving the school to a different responsible body with the track record and capacity to make improvements.

However, there is also room for the regulatory theory of change to provide additional levers through 'softer' interventions to support schools where performance does not require governance change. In essence, this is likely to necessitate the flow of expertise and capacity across organisational boundaries into schools that would benefit from such support.

Softer regulatory steps to foster school improvement are driven not by the isolated efforts of individuals but by the collective and strategic actions of organisations, particularly school trusts, coordinated at a regional level by the regulator.

The case study below offers an example of both hard and soft levers in action, where governance change was required but immediate improvement support was necessary. It reflects the fact that where endemic failure is identified in *any* type of school or structure, there should be an immediate response. It demonstrates the power of collaboration between regulators and the sector, and it shows how the system can be mobilised as a force for improvement.

The power of collaborative action to secure improvement

By Warren Carratt, chief executive of Nexus Multi Academy Trust, and Wayne Norrie, chief executive of Greenwood Academies Trust

The term partnership is used a lot in our state education system. Sometimes 'partnership' – and the pursuit of it – is incorrectly used to describe a situation where one individual (whether acting in their own interests or on behalf of an organisation they represent) wants something, and they need to use someone else to get it.

This is not partnership.

This transactional need is predicated on singular gain of the one over the many.

Instead, we believe that partnership in education should be defined as a relationship forged by the need for more than one party to come together in the interests of children. Where individual sacrifice is offset by collective gain and benefit. Where there is a clear pursuit of equity and improvement.

This is the understanding of partnership that we both brought to our work at the Evolve Trust.

Evolve Trust was a four-school trust (one secondary, one primary and two special schools), which had been ordered by the regulator to close one of its special schools – Harlow Academy – following significant safety concerns raised during an Ofsted inspection in January 2022.

Harlow was a school for children with severe and complex needs. Only 50% of its budget share was spent on staffing. The average is around 85% in similar schools, due to the acute medical needs of children. This meant that children were left in neglectful conditions where their safety could not be ensured.

The Ofsted report following the inspection in January 2022 said: 'Pupils are not safe in this school. Staff do their best to care and provide for the complex needs of pupils. But there are not enough staff to make sure that all pupils are properly cared for. The lack of staff leaves pupils at imminent risk of harm.'

The Nottinghamshire Safeguarding Children Partnership commissioned a lessons learned review. It concluded: 'The chronologies and reports from Nottinghamshire County Council and Nottinghamshire Healthcare Foundation Trust present a shocking picture of the decline of the quality of care of children at Harlow Academy in the months prior to the Ofsted inspection of January 2022. The decline was to a point where the school was not safe for the children.'

It was in this context that the Department for Education brought in two local trusts to respond to these failings. Nexus Multi Academy Trust was asked to provide interim leadership for Harlow Academy and oversee rapid improvement. Shortly afterwards, Greenwood Academies Trust was asked to provide interim leadership of the Evolve Trust, with a view to it being dissolved. Both commissions came with the need to understand the context urgently and build trust with families, multi-agency partners and the staff team across the trust.

Our shared priority at Harlow Academy was to reopen the school to children as quickly as we could. However, given the complex needs of the children the school served, this was not simple, as we had to recruit, train and induct new colleagues in order for us to be confident Harlow would be a safe, happy and caring environment for all children.

The second, and equally important, priority was to win back the trust of the families the school served. This was a long process, enabling parents and carers to manage anger, guilt and distress as a result of their children being in an environment where they were unsafe. This took the interim leadership teams at the trust and at Harlow a long time, leaving a powerful emotional legacy with them all.

The power of a partnership between two trusts with different specialisms but joined together by their values and moral purpose ensured that Harlow Academy began its journey to become the school it is today. It is unlikely, due to the extent of the issues at the school, that one trust alone would have the expertise and capacity to turn around Harlow as quickly as we did. We were most certainly stronger together.

At the heart of our partnership were the Principles of Public Life: selflessness, integrity, objectivity, accountability, openness, honesty and leadership. These seven principals permeated our work with each other as trusts and with the school and wider community. We used these principles to create the conditions for Harlow to thrive once again and for the system to keep getting better together, in collaboration not in competition.

This aligns with CST's broader vision for education, seeking a system that prioritises supportive, evidence-based and collaborative strategies in a way that is adaptive, resilient and attuned to the evolving needs of the local and national context.

We will achieve system improvement, as system leaders, through our collective acts of generosity, capacity-giving and reciprocity, as I have explored both in this chapter and in chapter twelve. These, too, are forms of radical collaboration where system leaders choose to act on the system rather than just in it, for the greater educational good of all schools and all children.

System architecture

Representative architecture

In the spring of 2022, I worked with Jonathan Simons at Public First to write a paper on how we build a mature institutional architecture in the English education system (Cruddas and Simons, 2022). This paper focused on public policymaking and the role of different national institutions in policymaking. The paper argued that most established professions have a stronger representative institutional architecture, typically comprising the following types of organisations:

- **Sector and employer bodies** are membership organisations that bring together, support and speak for organisations in a particular sector. The organisation, not an individual, is the member. Acting as the collective voice, sector bodies represent and promote the interests of the organisations they represent, and provide members with professional support and training. Sector bodies are also often employer bodies, and should be consulted on matters relating to employer functions and responsibilities.

- **Professional bodies** are organisations with individual members practising a profession in which the organisation maintains an oversight of the knowledge, skills, conduct and practice of that profession or occupation. Professional bodies cannot speak for employers as they represent individuals.

- **Trade unions** are organisations made up of individual members and this membership must be made up mainly of workers or employees. One of a trade union's main aims is to protect and advance the interests of its members in the workplace. By definition, trade unions cannot represent or speak on behalf of employers.

These organisations are *constitutionally representative*. Their governing documents (constitutions) set out the legitimate representative function they enact. Such organisations are permanent, derive authority and legitimacy because of their constitutional function, and have a wide range of interests in policy across a number of areas.

Government departments with responsibility for policy in areas of professional practice typically work with all types of institutional architecture organisations. It would be unthinkable, for example, for a regulator of the medical profession to form exclusive relationships with only a subset of these groups. This would be considered regulatory capture. In the established professions, the different national actors within the architecture have properly recognised roles and functions. Government, its departments and its regulators work appropriately with the full range of national organisations.

An important part of system leadership is the strengthening of the representative institutional architecture to ensure a balance of policy influence, but also to speak authoritatively to government on matters of policy. If we do not strengthen our institutional architecture, we will always be subject to the whims of governments, unable to exert proper professional influence.

Professional development architecture

I want to turn now to a different aspect of system architecture – the professional development architecture that supports teacher and leader development, and enables the system to keep getting better. This aspect of system architecture is fundamentally important because the evidence is clear that effects of high-quality teaching are especially significant for pupils from economically disadvantaged backgrounds: over a school year, these pupils gain 1.5 years' worth of learning with very effective teachers, compared to 0.5 years with poorly performing teachers (Sutton Trust, 2011). It also important because professions should have professional qualifications derived from, and explicitly focused on, professional standards.

In recent years, working with the Education Endowment Foundation, England has built the evidence base for high-quality teacher and leader development, and codified this in national frameworks like the early career framework and frameworks for national professional qualifications for teachers and leaders. In order to build system capacity, an institutional architecture has been developed to support this work. This includes a range of national providers[19] working with school trusts and teaching school hubs.[20]

There is also a network of subject hubs designed to develop expertise in teaching a specific subject or discipline, which complements the early career framework and national professional qualifications.

This system architecture enables a rich professional development landscape that has a mixture of rigorous professional qualifications, a broader regulated offer of professional development programmes, and highly frequent, contextualised learning opportunities in schools – all of which are increasingly informed by evidence. I believe the importance of this architecture is one of the key ways in which the state creates the conditions for systematic improvement. This is not just a collection of programmes that can be turned on and off, but an enduring feature of our improvement architecture.

This system architecture makes a fundamentally important contribution to our capacity to keep getting better as an education system, so that all our pupils can achieve and flourish. But it is not yet in an end state. So we need to work together to shape a national capacity-building system of organisations with the right roles and responsibilities, operating at the right scale. And we need the Treasury to understand and accept the economic and social value of education, the central importance of the quality of teaching and the role of professional development in improving the performance of our education system.

Evidence architecture

We are fortunate in England to have the Education Endowment Foundation, which is an independent charity dedicated to breaking the link between family income and educational achievement. The Education Endowment Foundation was founded in 2011 by the Sutton Trust in partnership with Impetus Trust (now part of Impetus – The Private Equity Foundation), with a £125 million founding grant from the Department for Education. It is part of the What Works Network, which uses evidence to improve the design and delivery of public services.

---

19 The national providers are Ambition Institute, Best Practice Network, Church of England, LLSE, National Institute of Teaching, Teacher Development Trust, Teach First, and University College London (UCL) Institute of Education.

20 Teaching school hubs are schools identified by the Department for Education as having capacity to offer teacher training and professional development. The vast majority of teaching school hubs are in school trusts. Teaching school hubs receive annual grant funding from the Department for Education.

The Education Endowment Foundation supports schools, colleges and early years settings to improve teaching and learning through better use of evidence. It generates, curates and disseminates research and evidence in education. It publishes synthesis reports and systematic reviews in areas where they do not currently exist. And it curates a network of research schools.

Research schools work with schools, colleges and early years settings in their regions to champion the use of evidence and improve teaching and learning, with a focus on socio-economically disadvantaged children and young people. They provide support to other schools by communicating research evidence, and supporting the translation of this into practice through training, exemplification and school-to-school support.

In addition to the Education Endowment Foundation, we are fortunate in England to have a number of national charities, like the National Foundation for Educational Research (NFER) and the Education Policy Institute (EPI), which form part of our evidence architecture.

Our representative architecture, professional development architecture and evidence architecture are all fundamentally important to an education system that has the capacity to keep getting better. We need now to build strong and accepted theories of education and a shared body of knowledge. In this, I think we still have quite a way to go. We are still near the beginning of our journey to establish this architecture so that it guides the work of educators in the way we see in other professions.

School trusts are a key part of this architecture. We need to continue to build a mature trust system with internal expertise to design and deliver high-quality professional learning, and the capabilities to make integrated, strategic use of national professional qualifications.

System governance

I want to turn now to system governance, which I think is the final piece in the rich and beautiful system architecture we are building.

Over the last few years, there has been a much contested debate about 'the middle tier'. This is an ill-defined concept, which in the end is probably meaningless. There are middle-tier functions – some of which are set out in legislation and others in custom and practice. However, even an analysis of these functions leads to a dead end of legacy thinking.

It is perhaps more helpful to consider what system governance might look like – and how we might construct governance of the system in a way that is intelligent, proportionate and coherent. A reset of system governance would set out the roles and responsibilities of all system actors.

As system leaders, we must call for, and co-construct, this system governance because it is an essential part of the way in which the system keeps getting better. As a minimum, this would involve clarity about:

- regulation
- inspection
- improvement.

Regulation

The state must be able to act (or intervene) quickly on behalf of children, parents and the wider public to ensure the highest quality of education, safety and safeguarding, and enforce regularity and propriety in the use of public money. However, the state does not need to exercise 'blunt' regulation in the form of intervention in order to protect high-quality education. Drawing on the work of Malcolm Sparrow (2020), regulation can be viewed as:

- the prevention of harms – or indeed the correction of harms
- the promotion of 'goods' – or perhaps differently worded, the promotion of high-quality education.

The state must retain the power (ultimately) to intervene in the most serious cases of poor-quality education or serious failures in safety and safeguarding. In these cases, the strong likelihood is a change of the governance of the school, or indeed the trust. But the state can also pursue a regulatory strategy that promotes high-quality education through some softer levers that support the improvement of a school. I address this in the next section.

Ultimately, I believe that regulation should be exercised in a way that is independent of government, by a single, expert regulator.

Inspection

In England the school inspectorate, Ofsted, has a legal duty to inspect schools, but Ofsted is not the regulator of schools. Ofsted inspections offer a view about the quality of education at a school at a point in time. While inspection can provide insight into where improvement is needed, improvement itself sits with responsible bodies.

Improvement

The responsibility for improving schools is, in my view, ultimately the role of the organisation with responsibility for those schools. In the case of schools working together as a group, it is the trust. This clarity of responsibility and accountability is very important and we should not muddle it. To do so is to undermine system governance.

The role of local government

In an emerging set of relationships, the role of local government is absolutely essential. I think there are three quite specific roles for local government.

1. **Protector:** Local government will always, in my view, exercise a protective function in relation to the most vulnerable children and young people. It will continue to have statutory duties in relation to safeguarding and children's social care. It must enact its duties as a 'corporate parent'. It will undoubtedly continue to have duties with regard to children and young people with special educational needs and disabilities. It must have a role in elective home education, children missing education, unaccompanied children and refugees.

2. **Convenor:** Local government has a very important convening function in relation to strategic objectives for education and the shaping of 'place' so that local areas are good places for children to grow up. It is important that local government has a convening role in the creation of social value and the promotion of public values. It has a sufficiency duty, as only the local authority will hold all the information required to calculate how many school places are needed.

3. **Supporter:** Local government has significant strategic capability and capacity. As such, it is important that it is able to work with education providers to help to overcome barriers and promote education as a social good. An example here would be the role of local government in supporting (and as a last resort, enforcing) school attendance. Another example would be to support the supply of teachers, particularly in areas where this is a local system-level problem. During the pandemic, we saw how local authorities have worked with trusts to enact civic leadership – addressing issues of public concern and place, and the protection and promotion of public values.

Concluding thoughts

If we can together get this system building right – if we can align system resilience, improvement, architecture and governance – we can perhaps finally create the conditions for our school system in England to keep getting better. It requires us to *see* the system. In chapter eight, I cited Senge *et al.* on the ability to see the larger system:

In any complex setting, people typically focus their attention on the parts of the system most visible from their own vantage point. This usually results in arguments about who has the right perspective on the problem. Helping people see the larger system is essential to building a shared understanding of complex problems. This understanding enables collaborating organisations to jointly develop solutions not evident to any of them individually and to work together for the health of the whole system rather than just pursue symptomatic fixes to individual pieces.

Senge, Hamilton and Kania (2015)

This aspect of system building will also require us to think hard, align system roles and responsibilities, make brave decisions and, as I wrote earlier in this chapter, make the case for investment so that the Treasury understands and accepts the economic and social value of education.

References

Cruddas, L. and Simons, J. (2022). *Building a mature institutional architecture in the English education system*. CST and Public First. Available at: https://cstuk. org.uk/knowledge/guidance-and-policy/building-a-mature-institutional-architecture-in-the-english-education-system-policies/.

Department for Education (2022). *The case for a fully trust-led system*. Available at: https://assets.publishing.service.gov.uk/media/62865295d3bf7f1f 433ae170/The_case_for_a_fully_trust-led_system.pdf.

Hosseini, S., Barker, K. and Ramirez-Marquez, J. (2016). 'A review of definitions and measures of system resilience', *Reliability Engineering and System Safety*, 145, 47–61.

National Audit Office (2021). *Principles of effective regulation*. Available at: https://www.nao.org.uk/wp-content/uploads/2021/05/Principles-of-effective-regulation-SOff-interactive-accessible.pdf.

Ofsted (2020). *Fight or flight? How 'stuck' schools are overcoming isolation: evaluation report*. Available at: https://www.gov.uk/government/publications/ fight-or-flight-how-stuck-schools-are-overcoming-isolation/fight-or-flight-how-stuck-schools-are-overcoming-isolation-evaluation-report.

Senge, P., Hamilton, H. and Kania, J. (2015). 'The dawn of system leadership', *Stanford Social Innovation Review*, Winter. Available at: https://ssir.org/ articles/entry/the_dawn_of_system_leadership#.

Sparrow, M. (2020). *Fundamentals of Regulatory Design*. Harvard University Press.

Sutton Trust, The (2011). *Improving the impact of teachers on pupil achievement in the UK: interim findings*. Available at: https://www.suttontrust.com/our-research/improving-impact-teachers-pupil-achievement-uk-interim-findings/.

CHAPTER FIFTEEN
BUILDING PUBLIC INSTITUTIONS

In this final chapter of this section on system leadership, I turn to building school trusts as public institutions. Just after the party conferences of 2023, I was invited to attend a dinner with vice chancellors at Queen Mary University of London, in its beautiful Old Library. Located in London's East End, a mile from the City of London, this is a university that is acutely aware of its civic role in place. All the vice chancellors who spoke that evening told profoundly moving stories of the places in which their universities are located and the civic role of universities. Sitting at that dinner, I had a moment of truly understanding what it means to build public institutions – and that it is possible to become too caught up in Westminster and political cycles.

Of course, we live in a democracy and it is fundamentally important that we respect the mandate that the state has in relation to state-funded education, including setting a public accountability framework for state schools. But it is also possible to think in longer terms than political cycles. This is because we are building public institutions, civic in their outlook, anchored in their communities.

In a fascinating paper on the subject of building institutions, Geoff Mulgan writes: 'Institutions exist because distinct tasks – running libraries, hospitals, armies, supporting science or providing welfare services – require a distinct ethos, methods and capabilities rather than generic bureaucracies' (Mulgan, 2024).

Part of the reason I am such a strong believer in school trusts is this fact – that they are specialist organisations set up for one purpose only: to run and improve our schools or, put another way, to advance education for public benefit. They do not have lots of other responsibilities in the way local authorities do. It seems to me that the education of our children is so important that it is desirable to have expert organisations responsible for our schools.

This does not mean for one minute that there is not a role for local government. Local government is an essential part of the enactment of democracy. In the previous chapter I set out what I believe the democratic roles and responsibilities for local government are.

Longevity, stickiness and purpose

Mulgan talks about the importance of longevity and stickiness. He identifies that many new institutions have indeed proved short-lived, and analyses why. He offers a view that while some were abolished for political symbolism,

perhaps too many had been set up to give the appearance of action rather than being based on sufficiently serious thought; perhaps too many used standard defaults, from NDPBs [non-departmental public bodies] and Executive Agencies to regulators, that weren't fit for purpose; and perhaps in too many cases the design focused solely on authority, finance and organograms, rather than issues of culture, intelligence or relationships.

Mulgan (2024)

In analysing the public institutions that have survived, Mulgan offers a view that, 'Some of the institutions which have survived longest combined a strong moral ethos and sense of mission along with competence and excellence. ... A tentative conclusion might be that some mix of moral purpose and mission, perceived competence and strong relationships is key to survival' (Mulgan, 2024). This is exactly what I have argued trusts are (or should be).

I believe the point about longevity is particularly important. Education policy is typically fiercely contested, and timelines are often foreshortened to each political cycle, each term of parliament. We live in a democracy, and it is important that we engage with parliamentarians and policy. Education policy and health policy are inextricably linked to government policy, if only because of public funding. But we also need to think in terms that are longer than the short-termism of political cycles.

This is how we build public institutions.

Centennials

I recently read Alex Hill's insightful book, *Centennials: The 12 Habits of Great, Enduring Organisations* (Hill, 2023). Hill offers a fascinating set of insights into organisations that have lasted a hundred years or more. He argues that their strategies for maintaining excellence and success frequently fly in the face of conventional wisdom.

A key premise of the book is 'stable core, disruptive edge'. The trust sector grew from a disruptive mindset and a key part of our success has been the ability to innovate. Now that more than 50% of pupils in England are educated in school trusts, it is perhaps easy (and desirable) to argue that trusts are part of the establishment. We are. We should hold on to this. And we should make the powerful, evidence-informed, values-driven case for all schools to be part of a strong and sustainable group working together in deep and purposeful collaboration in a single legal entity, with strong governance (the argument I put forward in chapter eleven).

But ... there is something unsettling in this. Yes, we want a stable core. Yes, we are part of the establishment, but we also need to continue to innovate. We need a disruptive edge.

Hill quotes Paul Thompson, the vice chancellor of the Royal College of Art, who says that the college is 'radically traditional': 'Out of this balance emerges the energy that propels them forward and a stability that ensures that no-one loses sight of what each centennial is there to achieve or forgets what has led to success in the past' (Hill, 2023, p. xv).

An interesting feature of Hill's disruptive edge is the habit of 'get better, not bigger'. This is controversial perhaps in our sector. So I just want to reinforce here a message from chapter one. Hill says that growth for centennials is something to be cautious about: 'They worry that the pursuit of growth at all costs can all too easily be a distraction from core goals and values. Excellence can change the world. Growth on its own won't' (Hill, 2023, p. 132).

Emerging design principles

Mulgan makes the important point that public institutions are, and should be, very diverse. He points out that past attempts to squeeze them into standardised forms often backfire. But he does point to some emerging design principles that he says can help to broaden the range and relevance of options. He highlights five principles that he says can help in the work of design (Mulgan, 2024):

Mulgan's emerging design principles

Dynamic metaphors

Different metaphors can guide design, so that instead of relying on traditional pyramids and classic organograms, alternatives can be drawn on including networks, flotillas, myceliums and other ideas taken both from nature and computer science rather than traditional public administration.

Shared intelligence

In the past the primary focus for institutional design was law and economics, or to put it another way, the organisation of authority and finance. These remain important but intelligence, data and knowledge are now increasingly central to the design of institutions, as they are in business. This includes not just what happens within institutions but also how they serve whole systems, ensuring that people, businesses and other organisations are supported with the intelligence they need to act successfully.

Meshes as well as silos

A related point is that governments are increasingly seeking ways of organising cross-cutting 'meshes' that allow 'whole of government' action, connecting multiple silos, multiple tiers, and multiple organisations, again often with shared knowledge.

Sparring and ecosystems

Institutions sit within a landscape or ecosystem – of cooperation, competition and challenge. No institution is an island. So, the work of design has to consider what surrounds the new institution, including how it may best be challenged so as to avoid complacency and stagnation.

More voice and inclusion

Finally, there is growing interest in new ways of organising voice and accountability – involving beneficiaries in shaping decisions and 'co-producing' services, and sometimes giving more formal power to communities, as well as tapping into much wider sources of expertise and collective intelligence.

Source: Mulgan (2024)

These design principles seem hugely important to the work of school trusts if we are to build public institutions that are fit for purpose into the future.

Building trust

This book has made the case for trust leaders to work with other civic leaders for the wider common good, and for trust leaders to act on the system rather than just in it.

Hill says: 'Centennials look at the whole of society, and every possibility, and ask themselves: "How can we shape how society thinks, and behaves, not only today, but for the next twenty to thirty years?"' (2023, p. 7). He cites Catherine Mallyon, the recent executive director of the Royal Shakespeare Company: 'If you don't positively shape society then, at some point, it will stop supporting you. At some point, it will stop wanting to work with you' (2023, p. 8).

We know that trust and confidence in public institutions is a concern right now. We see this in our schools through the problems with pupil attendance, behaviour and the exponential rise in parental complaints.

In chapter six I argued that the legitimacy of public institutions is crucial for building peaceful and inclusive societies. I cited the United Nations:

Trust is integral to the functioning of any society. Trust in each other, in our public institutions and in our leaders are all essential ingredients for social and economic progress, allowing people to cooperate with and express solidarity for one another. It allows public bodies to plan and execute policies and deliver services.

United Nations Department of Economic and Social Affairs (2021)

So, it is essential that, as public leaders, we work with our parents and communities to repair the social contract and to rebuild trust in schools as public institutions.

Building back

The 'Pisa 2022 national report for England' (Ingram *et al.*, 2023) gave us the stark and terrible finding that one in ten UK pupils reported that at least once a week they did not eat because there was not enough money to buy food. And we have seen recently from the Joseph Rowntree Foundation report, 'Destitution in the UK 2023', that there are now more than one million children in the UK living in destitution – that is, living without proper shelter or without enough food (Fitzpatrick *et al.*, 2023).

And in December 2023, UNICEF published a report which showed that child income poverty rates in the UK are the highest among the world's richest countries, and that we rank bottom of the table for changes in those rates in the past decade (Rees *et al.*, 2023, p. 27, Figure 14).

The government has estimated that 4.3 million children, or 30% of all children in the UK, were living in relative low-income households after housing costs in 2022/23. The percentage of children in absolute poverty has increased for the first time since 2018. After housing costs, the number of children living in absolutely poverty is 25% (Department for Work and Pensions, 2024).[21]

This is in the context of living in the world's sixth largest economy. It is unacceptable that position be allowed to continue.

To be clear, I do not think that public institutions, even working together in civic partnership, can solve the complex problem of poverty. It takes a committed government to pull the levers of state that will significantly reduce or eradicate child poverty.

It is worth returning to Lord Kerslake's prescient words from 2019 (which I cited in chapter six). The situation he described then is even more complex now, with greater implications for our public services and our public institutions. The deep economic and social changes that are happening in Britain today have made the civic role of public institutions even more vital – not just to the places they are located in, but in leading a response to the renewal of our communities and of civic life.

This requires something different of trust leaders as public leaders – it requires us to think in longer-term horizons and to build school trusts as public institutions. So perhaps the most important system leadership work is to build our trusts as public institutions advancing education for public benefit, civic in their outlook, anchored in their communities.

This is how we will build the resilience of our school system. It is how we will build back.

---

21   See in particular 'Section 7: Children in low-income households'.

References

Department for Work and Pensions (2024). *Households below average income: an analysis of the UK income distribution: FYE 1995 to FYE 2023.* Available at: https://www.gov.uk/government/statistics/households-below-average-income-for-financial-years-ending-1995-to-2023/households-below-average-income-an-analysis-of-the-uk-income-distribution-fye-1995-to-fye-2023#children-in-low-income-households.

Fitzpatrick, S., Bramley, G., Treanor, M., Blenkinsopp, J., McIntyre, J., Johnsen, S. and McMordie, L. (2023). *Destitution in the UK 2023.* Joseph Rowntree Foundation. Available at: https://www.jrf.org.uk/deep-poverty-and-destitution/destitution-in-the-uk-2023.

Hill, A. (2023). *Centennials: the 12 Habits of Great, Enduring Organisations.* Cornerstone Press.

Ingram, J., Stiff, S.J., Cadwallader, S., Lee, G. and Kayton, H. (2023). *Pisa 2022: national report for England.* Department for Education, Government Social Research. Available at: https://assets.publishing.service.gov.uk/media/656dc3321104cf0013fa742f/PISA_2022_England_National_Report.pdf.

Mulgan, G. (2024). *Designing new public institutions for the UK in the 2020s and beyond.* University College London and the Institutional Architecture Lab. Available at: https://www.geoffmulgan.com/post/designing-new-public-institutions-for-the-uk-in-the-2020s-and-beyond.

Rees, G., Timar, E., Dedewanou, F., Otchere, F., Carraro, A. and Cunsolo, S. (2023). *Child poverty in the midst of wealth* (Report Card 18). UNICEF. See figure 14, p. 27. Available at: https://www.unicef.org/innocenti/reports/child-poverty-midst-wealth#report.

United Nations (2021). *Trust in public institutions: trends and implications for economic security.* UN Department of Economic and Social Affairs. Available at: https://social.desa.un.org/publications/trust-in-public-institutions-trends-and-implications-for-economic-security.

AFTERWORD
AN OPEN LETTER TO SCHOOL
AND TRUST LEADERS

Dear Colleagues,

On 16 March 2020, I wrote my first Covid-19 email briefing to CST members. In that first message at the start of the pandemic, I thanked you for your leadership in uncertain and very worrying times. The last five years has also been a story of heroism and service and great courage.

However hard this is (and it has been very difficult for so much of the time), you have never stopped, not once, to put yourselves first. At every moment, you have done your civic duty.

You have done this because you believe in the power of education to improve lives – and indeed to change the world.

So I want to conclude this book with a personal message to you, through invoking the spirit of one of my favourite poems written by the great Maya Angelou. This poem exhorts us to *continue* – it is a soliloquy on perseverance, love and kindness.

Let us lead with perseverance - with the persistence and tenacity to do the right thing.

Let us lead with love and wisdom, that increases the spirit and cultivates human powers.

Let us lead with kindness and justice, unafraid to use the mantel of our protection.

And finally let us lead with quiet authority and compassion, seeking first to serve.

Our enduring and shared mission is to advance education for public benefit and create opportunity for all children. While this mission goes among things that change (governments, policies, legislation), it does not change. Let's never let go of this.

Warmest wishes,

Leora